Thomas Hardy
and British Poetry

Thomas Hardy and British Poetry

Donald Davie

Routledge & Kegan Paul
London

B1

First published in Great Britain in 1973
by Routledge & Kegan Paul Ltd
Broadway House, 68-74 Carter Lane,
London EC4V 5EL
Printed in Great Britain by
Unwin Brothers Limited
The Gresham Press, Old Woking, Surrey, England
A member of the Staples Printing Group
© Donald Davie 1972

ISBN 0 7100 7530 8

Contents

v

Acknowledgments

Leaving aside the people named in the text and footnotes, I am particularly conscious of a debt to members of graduate seminars that I have taught at Stanford on "British Poetry, 1870-1920" and on "British Poetry since Hardy." But my greatest obligation is certainly to my wife, Doreen Davie. All my books, whether in verse or prose, are in some important degree collaborations with her; but in the present venture, because I have been concerned with the temper of political sentiment in modern British society, I have been more than usually dependent on her to check my impressions, refine them, sometimes repudiate them. And beyond this there has also been, as always, her patience and her encouragement.

Quotations from *The Life of Thomas Hardy 1840-1928* by Florence Emily Hardy are used by permission of Macmillan London and Basingstoke. "Snow in the Suburbs," "A Spellbound Palace," "Louie," and "Green Slates" are reprinted by permission of The Macmillan Company from *Collected Poems* by Thomas Hardy, copyright 1925 by The Macmillan Company, renewed 1953 by Lloyds Bank, Ltd. Other verses by Hardy are reprinted by permission of The Macmillan Company from *Collected Poems* by Thomas Hardy, copyright 1925 by The Macmillan Company.

Poems and verses from *A Look Round the Estate*, copyright © 1962, 1967, by Kingsley Amis are reprinted by permission of Harcourt Brace Jovanovich Inc. Poems and verses from *John Betjeman's Collected Poems* are reprinted by permission of Sir John Betjeman and John Murray (Publishers) Ltd. "The night is freezing fast" by A. E. Housman is reprinted from *The Collected Poems of A. E. Housman*, copyright 1922 by Holt, Rinehart and Winston, Inc., copyright 1950 by Barclays Bank Ltd. Reprinted by permission of Holt, Rinehart and Winston, Inc.

Thanks are due to J. H. Prynne and Grosseteste Press for permission to quote from *The White Stones* by J. H. Prynne.

Quotations from W. H. Auden's Introduction to *Slick But Not Streamlined: Selected Writings of John Betjeman* are by permission of Sir John Betjeman. Quotations from poems by Roy Fisher are from *Collected Poems* (copyright © Roy Fisher 1969. Reprinted by permission of Fulcrum Press), and from *City* (copyright © Roy Fisher 1961. Reprinted by permission of Michael Shayer and Migrant Press).

Quotations from *The Complete Poems of D. H. Lawrence* are reprinted by permission of The Viking Press Inc. From *The Whitsun Weddings*, copyright 1969 by Philip Larkin, quotations are used by permission of Random House Inc.; as are quotations from *The Collected Poetry of W. H. Auden*, copyright 1945, from *The Shield of Achilles*, copyright 1955, *About the House*, copyright 1966, and *City Without Walls*, copyright 1969, all by W. H. Auden.

Quotations from *The Way of a World*, copyright 1969 by Charles Tomlinson, are used by permission of Oxford University Press London.

Foreword

I n this book I have taken it for granted that works of literary art
are conditioned by economic and political forces active in the society from which those works spring and to which they are directed,
forces which bear in on the solitary artist as he struggles to compose. And I have supposed further that the art-work has, or should
have, an effect in moulding the political actions and sentiments of
those who respond to it. These are not, I think, notions that origi-
nated with Karl Marx, though Marx valuably systematized them
and gave them a polemical edge. At all events they are now assumptions basic to any responsible literary history. Certainly they are not
the perquisite of the political left. For to accept these assumptions,
if it commits the literary historian to a loosely Marxist understanding of the past, does not commit him to accepting Marxist projec-
tions into a Messianic future, and hence not to leftist programs in
the politics of today.

Though this is a book about poetry, I devote a few pages to one
work which is not a poem, unless we concede—as why should we
not?—that some poems are written in prose. This is J. R. R. Tolkien's *Lord of the Rings*. I do not think that this is wayward or arbitrary on my part. There is evidence that, rightly or wrongly, this
work has attracted and delighted more readers than any work in
English verse since Eliot's *Waste Land*, and possibly more than any
work of imaginative prose over the same period. Its abiding appeal

was, it seemed to me, a phenomenon which I could not ignore without dishonesty in an attempt to define the political temper of the educated classes in England on the basis of the literature which they have produced and responded to in the last fifty years. To be sure, *The Lord of Rings* is often pointed to as a prime example of "pure" literature, "timeless," certainly without any implications of a political sort for contemporary England. But precisely its being recommended on those terms was a reason why it could not be overlooked in an inquiry undertaken on the assumption that such apolitical works are an impossibility. I am afraid my pages on *The Lord of the Rings* will offend many readers of that astonishing work. To them I will only suggest that if I argue for this romance as having, despite appearances, a consistent and pointed relevance to political thought and behavior in modern Britain, I am taking it more seriously, and giving more credit to its author, than they do who conceive it to be concerned only with such safely anachronistic matters as the divine right of kings.

The most obviously useful and valuable thing that criticism can do is demand attention for neglected talent. I wish I had found opportunities to do more of this. But I have invited recognition for two neglected talents, Roy Fisher and J. H. Prynne. If I do not couple with these names that of Charles Tomlinson, it is because the underrating and misunderstanding of Tomlinson are scandals of such long standing that, when I think of them, I despair.

Stanford, California   D.D.
January 1972

Introduction

The poems I am to discuss in the following pages have been chosen so as to illustrate a thesis: that in British poetry of the last fifty years (as not in American) the most far-reaching influence, for good and ill, has been not Yeats, still less Eliot or Pound, not Lawrence, but *Hardy*.

Pound, to be sure, unlike the others named, has declared himself among the beneficiaries of Hardy; and indeed there is need of an essay or a monograph that would map a way into the poetic universe of Pound by the firmly interlinked stages of an English route that runs from Landor to Hardy through Browning.[1] Such a study would necessarily swim against the ever more rapid current that is flowing nowadays in the commentaries toward what Daniel Pearlman hails with enthusiasm as "the *dehistoricization* of Pound."[2] For Hardy has the effect of locking any poet whom he influences into the world of historical contingency, a world of specific places at specific times. Vernon Watkins realized this, when he asserted that he and Dylan Thomas were both religious poets, who "could never write a poem dominated by time, as Hardy could."[3]

---

[1] See Pound's tribute to Hardy in *Confucius to Cummings*, ed. by Ezra Pound and Marcella Spann (New York, 1964), Appendix I.

[2] *Agenda*, 8, 3-4 (Autumn-Winter 1970), p. 6.

[3] *Letters to Vernon Watkins*, 1957, pp. 17-18, quoted by J. Press, *A Map of Modern English Verse* (London, 1969), p. 222. It is worth saying that not

3

Hardy appears to have mistrusted, and certainly leads other poets to mistrust, the claims of poetry to transcend the linear unrolling of recorded time. This is at once Hardy's strength and his limitation; and it sets him irreconcilably at odds with for instance Yeats, who exerts himself repeatedly to transcend historical time by seeing it as cyclical, so as to leap above it into a realm that is visionary, mythological, and (in some sense or to some degree) *eternal*. It ought to be possible for any reader to admire and delight in both Hardy and Yeats, if only because so much of the finest Yeats is concerned with the effort of transcendence rather than the achievement of it. But for any poet who finds himself in the position of choosing between these two masters, the choice cannot be fudged; there is no room for compromise. And so there is an emblematic significance to Philip Larkin's conversion (the word with its religious overtones seems not excessive) from Yeats to Hardy in 1946, after his very Yeatsian first collection, *The North Ship*.[4] Equally, there is perhaps tragic significance to the fact that Hardy is said to have been Dylan Thomas's favorite poet, whereas Yeats was his chosen master.

So much might be readily granted. To get beyond this point, we need to erase from our minds the image of (to use Henry James's unforgivable phrase) "the good little Thomas Hardy." None of Hardy's admirers have yet found how to make Hardy the poet

---

all poets who have been influenced by Hardy are prepared to acknowledge the fact, or are capable of recognizing it. This applies particularly to Irish, Scottish and Welsh poets, who do not care to be indebted to such an intransigently *English* poet as Hardy. Elizabeth Huberman (*The Poetry of Edwin Muir*, New York, 1971, pp. 54-56) is sure that Muir's *Chorus of the Newly Dead* (1926) is in many ways manifestly indebted to Hardy. And I remain impenitently convinced that I detect Hardy behind some early poems by Hugh MacDiarmid, though I have been reproved by Kenneth Buthlay for saying as much. It is hard to believe that the scientific humanism to which the Irishman Austin Clarke appears to vow himself in a poem such as "Medical Missionary of Mary" was arrived at without some appreciation of Hardy. And even R. S. Thomas, whose dismissal of Hardy serves as epigraph to my next chapter, seems to me markedly Hardyesque in for instance "The Conductor" (from *Tares*, 1961).

4 See his Introduction to the 1966 reprint of that book.

weigh equally with Eliot and Pound and Yeats, in the image we have of the world that not just poets, but English-speaking intellectuals generally, have inhabited through the last half-century. Affection for Hardy the poet is general, and quite often (in Britain, at any rate) it is fervent; but it is ruinously shot through with protectiveness, even condescension. Hardy is not thought of as an intellectual force. When he is, rarely, considered from that point of view, it has been customary to say that whereas, as an imagination, he survives to instruct and challenge us, as an intellect he is *dated*, set into a late Victorian mould which the twentieth century finds not just outmoded but irrelevant. Herbert Spencer and Thomas Henry Huxley are old hat; and Hardy, who formed his ideas in the same climate of opinion, is therefore out of date. But quite apart from the question whether a man's images can be divorced from his ideas quite so cleanly (if they can, either the human imagination is being downgraded, or else the human intellect is), the second half of the twentieth century is surely much less confident than the first half was, of having outgrown Thomas Henry Huxley. The scientific humanism to which Huxley and Hardy gave their allegiances survives as a working ethic. The Second World War, which so discredited the reactionary or religious alternatives that had been promoted by the poets and the literary intellectuals, shook also—for instance, in the Oppenheimer case—the confidence of the scientific humanists, but not so radically. If "we are all socialists now," we are all by that token scientific humanists also; and to just that degree the ideas of Thomas Hardy, even if we bitterly oppose them, are far more forces to be reckoned with than the ideas of T. S. Eliot. And political stances quite far to the right of programmatic socialism are scientific-humanist no less. In the academies, the literary intellectual who in his classroom toys with the antidemocratic opinions of a Pound or Yeats or Wyndham Lewis, Lawrence or Eliot, transforms himself into a social democrat as soon as he attends his university senate, voting there, and perhaps speaking eloquently, in favor of "freedom of inquiry"—a principle which his authors regarded without enthusiasm, if not indeed with animosity, much as some of them profited by it. And in standing by that principle, though he may call on authorities as old as Erasmus and Montaigne, the literary man knows that in a university senate, or a state senate either for that matter, the effective force behind it, which he needs to muster, is the ethic of the laboratory. In that way, scientific humanism is the ethic behind not just socialist positions in politics, but equally behind all those which may be called, or may call themselves, liberal.

Indeed, in all the worryings which in recent years have become so common, about the illiberal social and political ideas of the great literary imaginations of the present century (Pound and Eliot, Yeats and Lawrence), it is remarkable that to my knowledge no one has cited Hardy as the exception that proves the rule. For it could well be argued that Hardy is the one poetic imagination of the first magnitude in the present century who writes out of, and embodies in his poems, political and social attitudes which a social democrat recognizes as "liberal." To take only one example, and incidentally to reveal liberalism in politics at its most vulnerable, Hardy's response to the First World War seems to have been liberal in a sense which does little credit to his shrewdness. The war seems to have taken him completely by surprise. Skeptical as he was in general, or was taken to be, he appears to have believed that European man, enlightened as he had been by scientific liberalism, had progressed beyond the point at which he would any longer have recourse to war. His less liberal and more coarse-grained contemporary, Rudyard Kipling, knew better—as of course did any number of observant journalists, who had seen the arms race gather momentum, and the balance of power tilt. But of international politics at that measurable and observable level Hardy appears to have been quite innocent—as the liberal tends to be.

He rallied from the shock of the war, and tried to make sense of it retrospectively, in a document which is central to my purpose. This is the "Apology" (dated: "February 1922"), with which he prefaced his post-war collection, *Late Lyrics and Earlier*.

Hardy had no talent for discursive prose, and this document cannot be read without exasperation. The trouble is not simply lack of talent for the marshaling and conduct of an argument. The way in which *Tess of the D'Urbervilles* and *Jude the Obscure* were received had rankled with Hardy over the years. And some of the discontinuities in the "Apology" seem to represent an attempt to outwit and hoodwink the reader whom Hardy rancorously envisages. He wants to insinuate his argument so as to disarm the prejudices which he believes it would inflame were he to state it openly. A maneuver so complicated called upon urbane skills which Hardy did not possess; and his dislike and distrust of his readers peep through unattractively. For all these reasons, much of the piece is as if written in a clumsy code which we have to break. However, it is in its tortuous way explicit enough, at the point where he addresses the select few who will not mistake his "evolutionary meliorism" for "pessimism":

> looking down the future these few hold fast to the same: that whether the human and kindred animal races survive till the exhaustion or destruction of the globe, or whether these races perish and are succeeded by others before that conclusion comes, pain to all upon it, tongued or dumb, shall be kept down to a minimum by loving-kindness, operating through scientific knowledge, and actuated by the modicum of free will conjecturally possessed by organic life when the mighty necessitating forces—unconscious or other—that have "the balancings of the clouds," happen to be in equilibrium, which may or may not be often.

The last part of this inelegant sentence makes it forgivable to think of Hardy, even today, as a pessimist; for introduction of the words, "free will," and the immediate mournful qualification of them in clause after clause, phrase after phrase, mirror quite comically how in Hardy's system there is indeed a margin for human choice but the slimmest margin imaginable. Cramped and intermittent as that area of freedom may be, Hardy, however, is quite clear about what should motivate our actions within it—it is "loving-kindness, operating through scientific knowledge." This is what I have meant so far and shall mean in what follows, by "scientific humanism."

Why Hardy thought the position worth restating, and the plea worth making, appears near the end of the essay when, speaking of "poetry, pure literature in general, religion,"[5] he declares:

> these, I say, the visible signs of mental and emotional life, must like all other things keep moving, becoming; even though at present, when belief in witches of Endor is displacing the Darwinian theory and "the truth that shall make you free," men's minds appear . . . to be moving backwards rather than on.

If we remember Yeats's *A Vision* (1925) or *Per Amica Silentia Lunae* (1917) or Lawrence's *Fantasia of the Unconscious* (1922), we may be forgiven for associating them with that "belief in witches of Endor" which Hardy, as a Darwinian, regards with such contempt and dismay.

The hidden or "encoded" message of the piece supports this explicit message. The key to it is something to which Hardy himself draws attention, the extent to which the "Apology" is interlarded with quotations from Wordsworth, some of them dragged in by the ears, others conspicuously "wrenched." The reason appears when we come to the last of them, when Hardy confesses to

> a forlorn hope, a mere dream, that of an alliance between religion, which must be retained unless the world is to perish, and complete rationality, which must come, unless also the world is to perish, by means of the interfusing effect of poetry—"the breath and finer spirit of all knowledge; the impassioned expression of science," as it was defined by an English poet who was quite orthodox in his ideas.

What is alluded to is a famous passage among those which Wordsworth added to the Preface to *Lyrical Ballads,* for the edition of 1802. Familiar though it is (or should be), I shall give it in full:

[5] Hardy's uncharacteristic tenderness toward "religion" in this essay—and institutional religion at that, as the context makes clear—derives from short-lived hopes he entertained at this time for "modernism" in the Church of England. See *The Life of Thomas Hardy, 1840-1928,* by Florence Emily Hardy (London, 1962), p. 415. (This "ghosted" autobiography by Hardy appeared first in two separate volumes, *The Early Life of Thomas Hardy, 1840-1891* (1928), and *The Later Years of Thomas Hardy, 1892-1928* (1930)).

The knowledge both of the Poet and the Man of Science is pleasure; but the knowledge of the one cleaves to us as a necessary part of our existence, our natural and inalienable inheritance; the other is a personal and individual acquisition, slow to come to us, and by no habitual and direct sympathy connecting us with our fellow-beings. The Man of Science seeks truth as a remote and unknown benefactor; he cherishes and loves it in his solitude: the Poet, singing a song in which all human beings join with him, rejoices in the presence of truth as our visible friend and hourly companion. Poetry is the breath and finer spirit of all knowledge: it is the impassioned expression which is in the countenance of all Science. Emphatically may it be said of the Poet, as Shakespeare hath said of man, "that he looks before and after." He is the rock of defence of human nature; an upholder and preserver, carrying every where with him relationship and love. In spite of difference of soil and climate, of language and manners, of laws and customs, in spite of things silently gone out of mind and things violently destroyed, the Poet binds together by passion and knowledge the vast empire of human society, as it is spread over the whole earth, and over all time. The objects of the Poet's thoughts are everywhere; though the eyes and senses of man are, it is true, his favorite guides, yet he will follow wheresoever he can find an atmosphere of sensation in which to move his wings. Poetry is the first and last of all knowledge—it is as immortal as the heart of man. If the labours of men of Science should ever create any material revolution, direct or indirect, in our condition, and in the impressions which we habitually receive, the Poet will sleep then no more than at present, but he will be ready to follow the steps of the Man of Science, not only in those general indirect effects, but he will be at his side, carrying sensation into the midst of the objects of the Science itself. The remotest discoveries of the Chemist, the Botanist, or Mineralogist, will be as proper objects of the Poet's art as any upon which it can be employed, if the time should ever come when these things shall be familiar to us, and the relations under which they are contemplated by the followers of these respective Sciences shall be manifestly and palpably material to us as enjoying and suffering beings. If the time should ever come when what is now called Science, thus familiarized to men, shall be ready to put on, as it were, a form of flesh and blood, the Poet will lend his divine spirit to aid the transfiguration, and will welcome the Being thus produced, as a dear and genuine inmate of the household of man.

Hardy's strategy was, we now realize, to buttress his case for scientific humanism as the only respectable working ethic for the poet, by enlisting as a scientific humanist *avant la lettre* an authority much more compelling than his own could be, bedeviled as his was (so he believed) by willful misrepresentations of his own position as perversely "unorthodox." The elaborateness of the maneuver, however clumsily executed, shows how much Hardy took this cause to heart.

Yet if the buoyancy and generous certainty of Wordsworth's eloquence show up Hardy's manifesto as, by contrast, cramped and undermined by melancholy, it shows up hardly less damagingly the other literary authority from the nineteenth century whom Hardy cites: Matthew Arnold. For Hardy in his "Apology" twice endorses Arnold's definition of poetry as "the application of ideas to life." And one virtue of Wordsworth's expansive but carefully indefinite formulations is that they leave room for relations between Science and Poetry altogether more intimate and less mechanical than the "application" of the ideas of the one to the subject matter of the other. Hardy's most obviously Darwinian or post-Darwinian poems suffer from answering all too patly to Arnold's formula, disregarding the more intimate alliances with the sciences such as Wordsworth allowed for. (These were left for Hugh MacDiarmid to explore.)

On the other hand, the affirmative expansiveness of Wordsworth's welcome to the sciences, though appropriate to the first decade of the nineteenth century (when, however, the appropriateness was apparent only to unusually perceptive men, such as Wordsworth was), would have been quite out of place in the third decade of the present century, except for people much more unfeeling and much less perceptive than Thomas Hardy. Hardy had seen, and had documented in a dozen novels and many poems, the strains and the outright damage which applied science, through industrialization and urbanization, had inflicted on the fabric of social and interpersonal relationships in the England that he knew. Indeed, sympathetic and perceptive readers have before now seen Hardy's entire career, in novels and poems alike, as an elegiac and indignant celebration of pre-industrial values which industrial technology had doomed.[6] In fact, I believe and hope to show that Hardy's attitudes were a great deal more complicated than that, and more ambiguous. For instance, "The Convergence of the Twain," which some of us like to remember as a condemnation of technological presumption, in fact very markedly censures the vanity and luxury which created and inhabited the staterooms of the ocean liner, but not the technology which built the great ship and navigated her. Moreover, Raymond Williams has shown[7] that Hardy was well aware how the English peasantry, and the less fortunate among the yeomanry also, had been debased into an agricultural proletariat already, long before he was born. Thus, if Hardy finally pins what hopes he has upon science, and upon the industrial technology which is science's concomitant, he does so in full knowledge of a human cost which he has counted. And this ought to mean that Hardy speaks to these crucial issues with a weight and an authority perhaps greater than that of any imaginative writer of English, of comparable seriousness, in the present century. On the other hand, we have already come across grounds for thinking that Hardy will speak to these issues most cogently when he is concerned overtly with something quite different. Other things being equal, we should be prepared to listen to a Hardy poem most attentively when it is furthest from answering patly to Arnold's formula: the application of ideas to life. Hardy's attitude to technology will appear clearly, not from what he says about it (in his poems as a whole he says little), but from the formal dispositions of and in his verse style. His scientific humanism will be most influential on other poets, not as a set of propositions or a manifesto, but as an attitude informing his practice of his art.

Some of the features of later British poetry which have baffled and offended readers, especially in America—I have in mind an apparent meanness of spirit, a painful modesty of intention, extremely limited objectives—fall into place if they are seen as part

[6] See Douglas Brown, *Thomas Hardy* (London, 1954).

[7] Raymond Williams, "Thomas Hardy," in *The Critical Quarterly*, 6.4 (Winter 1964), pp. 341-51.

of an inheritance from Hardy, an attempt to work out problems, especially social and political problems, which Hardy's poetry has posed for the twentieth century. And I hope to do more than merely excuse these characteristics of writing in the Hardyesque tradition; I want to present them as challenging, and to ask in effect, "Are not Hardy and his successors right in severely curtailing for themselves the liberties that other poets continue to take? Does not the example of the Hardyesque poets make some of those other poets look childishly irresponsible?"

～ 1 ～

Hardy
as Technician

Then Hardy, for many a major
Poet, is for me just an old stager,
Shuffling about a bogus heath,
Cob-webbed with his Victorian breath.[1]

Hardy's poetry is a body of writing before which one honest critic after another has by his own confession retired, baffled and defeated. It is nothing short of comical that a criticism which can make shift to come to terms with Ezra Pound or Apollinaire, Charles Olson or René Char, should have to confess itself unable to appraise with confidence a body of verse writing like Hardy's, which at first glance offers so much less of a challenge to tested assumptions and time-honored procedures. Irving Howe's confession is admirably explicit:

> Any critic can, and often does, see all that is wrong with Hardy's poetry, but whatever it was that makes for his strange greatness is much harder to describe. Can there ever have been a critic of Hardy who, before poems like "The Going" and "During Wind and Rain," did not feel the grating inadequacy of verbal analysis, and the need to resort to such treacherous terms as "honesty," "sincerity," and even "wisdom"?[2]

[1] R. S. Thomas, "Taste," *Poetry Review*, 1970.
[2] Irving Howe, *Thomas Hardy* (New York, 1967), p. 164.

13

Unless he has felt as Irving Howe describes, no critic of Hardy's poetry is qualified to speak. Equally, for the mere honor of the critical vocation, no one has the right to publish yet another essay on Hardy unless he thinks he can transpose the discussion into other terms than those which Howe rightly calls "treacherous." I write in that hope, or under that delusion.

Yvor Winters declared that Hardy was, "like Emily Dickinson, essentially a naif, a primitive, but one of remarkable genius."[3] Yet neither "naïve" nor "primitive" is the word that comes first to mind to characterize the most elaborate and considered of Hardy's few statements about his understanding of his own art. The statement is made in the third person because it comes from the very reticent autobiography which Hardy "ghosted" through his second wife:[4]

> In the reception of this [Wessex Poems] and later volumes of Hardy's poems there was, he said, as regards form, the inevitable ascription to ignorance of what was really choice after full knowledge. That the author loved the art of concealing art was undiscerned. For instance, as to rhythm. Years earlier he had decided that too regular a beat was bad art. He had fortified himself in his opinion by thinking of the analogy of architecture, between which art and that of poetry he had discovered, to use his own words, that there existed a close and curious parallel, both arts, unlike some others, having to carry a rational content inside their artistic form. He knew that in architecture cunning irregularity is of enormous worth, and it is obvious that he carried on into his verse, perhaps in part unconsciously, the Gothic art-principle in which he had been trained—the principle of spontaneity, found in mouldings, tracery, and such like—resulting in the "unforeseen" (as it has been called) character of his metres and stanzas, that of stress rather than of syllable, poetic texture rather than poetic veneer; the latter kind of thing, under the name of "constructed ornament", being what he, in common with every Gothic student, had been taught to avoid as the plague. He shaped his poetry accordingly, introducing metrical pauses, and reversed beats; and found for his trouble that some particular line of a poem exem-

[3] Yvor Winters, *Forms of Discovery* (Chicago, 1967), p. 189.
[4] *The Life of Thomas Hardy, 1840-1928*, pp. 300-301.

plifying this principle was greeted with a would-be jocular remark
that such a line "did not make for immortality."

One may believe that this is a wrongheaded or foolish way of considering poetry, as is (so some think) any consideration of one art
by analogy with another or with others. But in that case, surely,
one regards it as oversophisticated, not "primitive." And right or
wrong, this way of looking at the arts was not an eccentric quirk
in Hardy, but was shared by his contemporaries, including those,
like Pater and Hopkins and Patmore, whose education had been
both extensive and orthodox. Too much has been made of Hardy's
provincialism, and his being self-educated; people still treat him
with a sort of patronizing indulgence on these false grounds, very
much in the way that Hardy himself resented when he looked
through the eyes of Jude Fawley.[5] If Hardy was self-educated, the
education that he gave himself was in the end enviably thorough;
and if for instance we cannot make much use of the distinction
Hardy made in the passage just quoted, it is because *our* education has been neglected, and has not included those texts of Pugin
and Ruskin which Hardy and Patmore took for granted when they
talked about the aesthetic of Gothic architecture. Nor is this the
only field in which Hardy shames our ignorance; as a prosodist, for
instance, he was immensely learned, with a learning that seems to
be lost beyond recovery.

All the same, we should not fly to the other extreme. The autodidact *does* suffer, when set beside the man whose education has
come to him without struggle against circumstance. My guess is
that the autodidact suffers most from having had to discipline himself to depend too heavily on his own will, his own resolve to outwit circumstance and overcome it. And this is a very important
element in Hardy's personality. Though he struck those who met
him as a gentle and retiring man, the facts of his literary career

---

[5] See, for instance, Samuel Hynes: "Hardy went about the business of be-
coming a literary man with almost comic seriousness, like a burlesque of
Milton at Horton." (*The Pattern of Hardy's Poetry* (Chapel Hill, 1961),
p. 21.) I perceive nothing comic, nothing of "burlesque."

speak for themselves: it is a Victorian success story, a model career
on the lines of Samuel Smiles's self-help, with all that that involves
of driving oneself hard with grim and clenched determination.
And sometimes this is what offends us in Hardy's poetry—its form
mirrors a cruel self-driving, a shape *imposed* on the material, as it
were with gritted teeth. Edmund Blunden says something like this
when he remarks: "The faults of Hardy's verse are seldom those of
the mediocre man, with his apparently easy measures, never quite
full measures; they are those of a zealous experimenter, whose ma-
terials do not always obey the purpose or yield a restful completeness."[6] An example is "Lines to a Movement in Mozart's E-Flat
Symphony":

> Show me again the time
> When in the Junetide's prime
> We flew by meads and mountains northerly!—
> Yea, to such freshness, fairness, fulness, fineness, freeness,
>   Love lures life on.
>
> Show me again the day
> When from the sandy bay
> We looked together upon the pestered sea!
> Yea, to such surging, swaying, sighing, swelling, shrinking,
>   Love lures life on.
>
> Show me again the hour
> When by the pinnacled tower
> We eyed each other and feared futurity!—
> Yea, to such bodings, broodings, beatings, blanchings, blessings,
>   Love lures life on.
>
> Show me again just this:
> The moment of that kiss
> Away from the prancing folk, by the strawberry-tree!—
> Yea, to such rashness, ratheness, rareness, ripeness, richness,
>   Love lures life on.

Despite such incidental, characteristically audacious felicities as
"the pestered sea," this is surely not a poem we can admire. The

---

[6] Edmund Blunden, *Thomas Hardy* (London, 1942), ch. 12.

musical air, as in a song, imposes the stanzaic symmetry; the air is sounded four times over, with only minimal change. But the rigidly symmetrical correspondence of the fourth lines in the stanzas, a symmetry rammed home by heavy-handed alliteration, was not required by the music of Mozart, but has been imposed by the poet. And the heavy-handedness drives any lived experience out of sight beneath the verbal surface. Where here is the "cunning irregularity"? It is precisely what the poem needs, and suffers from the lack of. What one hears is not the chip-chip of a mason's chisel, but a clank of iron girders swung down from a crane; not Gothic architecture at all but specifically Victorian architecture, the iron bridges and railway stations of engineers like Brunel and Smeaton, who were indeed the accepted heroes of the self-help ethos. What destroys such a poem (and there are others like it) is not an all too stolidly planted rural provincialism, but just the opposite—its effective aesthetic is that of industrial technology in the age of heavy engineering. There is an essay to be written about Hardy the upwardly mobile *déraciné*; instead what we hear on every side is "Hardy the countryman."

It is Hardy the poet of technology, the laureate of engineering, who writes one of his most dazzling compositions, the poem on the sinking of the *Titanic*. The poem itself is an engine, a sleek and powerful machine; its rhymes slide home like pistons inside cylinders, ground exactly to fractions of a millimeter.

A more curious case from this point of view is a poem that Yvor Winters singled out, "The Wind's Prophecy":

> I travel on by barren farms
> And gulls glint out like silver flecks
> Against a cloud that speaks of wrecks,
> And bellies down with black alarms.
> I say: "Thus from my lady's arms
> I go: those arms I love the best!"
> The wind replies from dip and rise,
> "Nay; toward her arms thou journeyest."
>
> A distant verge morosely gray
> Appears, while clots of flying foam

Break from its muddy monochrome,
And a light blinks up far away.
I sigh: "My eyes now as all day,
Behold her ebon loops of hair!"
Like bursting bonds the wind responds,
"Nay, wait for tresses flashing fair!"

From tides the lofty coastlands screen
Come smitings like the slam of doors,
Or hammerings on hollow floors,
As the swell cleaves through caves unseen.
Say I: "Though broad this wild terrene,
Her city home is matched of none!"
From the hoarse skies the wind replies:
"Thou shouldst have said her sea-bord one."

The all-prevailing clouds exclude
The one quick timorous transient star;
The waves outside where breakers are
Huzza like a mad multitude.
"Where the sun ups it, mist-imbued,"
I cry, "there reigns the star for me!"
The wind outshrieks from points and peaks:
"Here, westward, where it downs, mean ye!"

Yonder the headland, vulturine,
Snores like old Skrymer in his sleep,
And every chasm and every steep
Blackens as wakes each pharos-shine.
"I roam, but one is safely mine,"
I say. "God grant she stay my own!"
Low laughs the wind as if it grinned:
"Thy love is one thou'st not yet known."

The grimness of this poem is quite extraordinary when we realize
that the westward journey it describes is the one on which, in 1870,
Hardy unexpectedly found his bride, Emma Gifford—the same
journey, in fact, that produced the sweet lilt, "When I set out for
Lyonnesse." It's true of course that the poem was almost certainly
written long afterwards, when the marriage had turned out badly.
What is uncanny is the way the elements are made to menace the

traveler, and through associations with technology—the gulls "glint" with a metallic glitter; when the sea comes into sight, its "muddy monochrome" has a hint of the daguerreotype; and when the sea passes out of sight, the sound it makes is a slamming and a hammering. These industrial associations gather until we wonder whether the huzza-ing multitude of the penultimate stanza is not a dangerously mercurial proletariat. We know that Hardy was capable of such disparaging sentiments about the masses. In 1891 he had written in his diary something which he transcribed for his ghosted autobiography:

> Next day—wet—at the British Museum: "crowds parading and gaily traipsing round the mummies, thinking today is for ever, and the girls casting sly glances at the young men across the swathed dust of Mycerinus (?) They pass with flippant comments the illuminated MSS.—the labours of years—and stand under Rameses the Great, joking. Democratic government may be justice to man, but it will probably merge in proletarian, and when these people are our masters it will lead to more of this contempt, and possibly to the utter ruin of art and literature! . . . Looking, when I came out, at the Oxford Music Hall, an hour before the time of opening, there was already a queue."[7]

This is something that should be kept in mind when reading the poem written many years later, "In Time of 'The Breaking of Nations' ":

> Yonder a maid and her wight
> Come whispering by:
> War's annals will fade into night
> Ere their story die.

The maid's and her wight's indifference to history is a fact; it is not necessarily reassuring. And as from Forster, so from Hardy, *two* cheers is all that Democracy deserves.

But in any case Lois Deacon's and Terry Coleman's revelations

[7] *The Life of Thomas Hardy, 1840-1928,* p. 236.

about Hardy's life,[8] up to the point where those eager sleuths launch into frailly supported speculation, throw a quite different light on "The Wind's Prophecy," and explain its otherwise inexplicable urgency and ominousness. (And it may as well be said here at once that, whatever the rights or wrongs of using biographical information to assist explication of other poets, in the case of an author so secretive as Hardy it has already proved itself indispensable.) They show conclusively that we read the poem right when we see it as dealing with Hardy's love for Tryphena Sparks, his cousin who in the end rejected him after he had see-sawed between her and Emma Gifford. Tryphena is the dark-haired girl behind the traveler eastward, whom he thinks of as his chosen; Emma is the blonde who, unknown to him, awaits him at his destination, St. Juliot in Cornwall. Tryphena is a woman of his own social station exactly; Emma, whether or not Hardy thought her a cut above him socially, certainly herself thought she was, and, as we know, regarded Hardy's marriage to her as a significant stage in his bettering of himself.[9] Thus the opposition between the two women, and the "fated" switch from one to the other—matters that are explicitly at the center of the poem—bring with them irrational feelings of guilt on the part of one who, upwardly mobile, is by that token "a class-traitor." And this explains much of the anxiety and foreboding which hang about the poem, otherwise unaccountably. But we may go, though hesitantly, a little further still, to account for the technological images. As we now read the poem, it is as if what separated Hardy from Tryphena were the Industrial Revolution itself, or at least as if the Nature which divided them (their relationship by blood was Tryphena's pretext for rejecting him) were itself a massive machine, of which sea and

---

[8] Lois Deacon and Terry Coleman, *Providence and Mr. Hardy* (London, 1966). Miss Deacon and Mr. Coleman prove that there was an affair with Tryphena; in my view they fail to prove that Tryphena bore a child to Hardy.

[9] See *Some Recollections by Emma Hardy*, ed. by Evelyn Hardy and Robert Gittings (London and New York, 1961). This indispensable and charming book had by 1970 been allowed to go out of print.

land and sky were components. And indeed, in a poem Hardy wrote about Tryphena's daughter after Tryphena died, Nature's manipulation of genetics is called "her mechanic artistry," and the generation of children is seen as a sort of metallurgy:

> But niggard Nature's trick of birth
> Bars, lest she overjoy,
> Renewal of the loved on earth
> Save with alloy.[10]

The same trope—"Every desired renewal of an existence is debased by being half alloy"—appears in *Jude the Obscure*, in what is, as Deacon and Coleman point out, an exactly parallel passage. Thus, one way to explain and vindicate the hoarse menace of "The Wind's Prophecy" is to say that, whatever Hardy consciously meant to convey about the forces which drove him from Tryphena to Emma, his imagery presents them as the pressures of an advanced technological society. However Victorian man may have harnessed wind and sea ("as wakes each pharos-shine"), those elemental energies will retort "like bursting bonds," and take their revenge where he can least resist them, in his sex and his sexual life. And in a devious remote way this is accurate enough about the relation between the young Hardy and his kinswoman Tryphena, as Deacon and Coleman permit us to reconstruct it. For Tryphena was no more the Dorset peasant than was her famous cousin. Like Sue Bridehead of *Jude the Obscure*, for whom in part Tryphena seems to have sat as model, Tryphena too was *déracinée*—having "bettered herself" as her cousin had done, making herself a London-trained schoolmistress at just the time when the Education Act of 1870 was recognizing the need, in an advanced technological culture, for virtually all the population to be, at an unambitious level, lettered and numerate.

Of course this is special pleading. The technological references in the poem are not so unambiguous, nor so insistent, as I have

---

[10] This poem first appeared in *Wessex Poems* (1898) as "To An Orphan Child. A Whimsey." It appears in *The Collected Poems of Thomas Hardy* (London, 4th edition 1930) p. 58, as "To a Motherless Child."

made out. And if this is, so far as I can see, the only way of reading the poem which accounts for all its components, the poem itself does not ask to be put together in this way. It is our reconstruc-
tion, as readers; the poem delivers to us, not an experience, but
only the components of an experience—and indeed not all of those.
Thus it fails to satisfy; and our interest in it is clinical.

A much better piece, yet one that still falls short of assured
achievement, is "Overlooking the River Stour":

> The swallows flew in the curves of an eight
> > Above the river-gleam
> > In the wet June's last beam:
> Like little crossbows animate
> The swallows flew in the curves of an eight
> > Above the river-gleam.
>
> Planing up shavings of crystal spray
> > A moor-hen darted out
> > From the bank thereabout,
> And through the stream-shine ripped his way;
> Planing up shavings of crystal spray
> > A moor-hen darted out.
>
> Closed were the kingcups; and the mead
> > Dripped in monotonous green,
> > Though the day's morning sheen
> Had shown it golden and honeybee'd;
> Closed were the kingcups; and the mead
> > Dripped in monotonous green.
>
> And never I turned my head, alack,
> > While these things met my gaze
> > Through the pane's drop-drenched glaze,
> To see the more behind my back. . .
> O never I turned, but let, alack,
> > These less things hold my gaze.

The "cunning irregularity" which heedless readers have taken for
clumsiness may be in a touch like the crowded stresses and conso-
nants in "the pane's drop-drenched glaze." But once we have taken
Hardy's word for it that such effects are the result of "choice after
full knowledge," the poem becomes throughout, and all too shin-

ingly, the work of "a superb technician" who dismays us precisely by his *superbia*. The symmetries, stanza by stanza, are all but exact to begin with; once we know that the occasional inexactitude is no less engineered, "engineered" seems more than ever the only word to use. Once again there is an analogy with Victorian civil engineering, which topped off an iron bridge or a granite waterworks with Gothic finials, just as Hardy tops off his Victorian diction with an archaism like "sheen" or "alack." Within its historically appropriate idiom, the poem is "a precision job"; that is to say, its virtuosity is of a kind impossible before conditions of advanced technology.

Just this indeed could be the grounds on which to claim that Hardy, in a poem like this, is a very great poet indeed. Where else, we might ask, do we find among Hardy's contemporaries an imagination which has grasped with comparable force—not in what it says, but in how it addresses itself to the act of composition—the essential nature and life style of late-Victorian England, an England which rested on mechanical technology, on heavy engineering? I think this is the probably unanswerable case that should and must be made for "The Convergence of the Twain." If the same case cannot be made for "Overlooking the River Stour," it is because its precision is more apparent than real. The poem raises issues which in the end it does not resolve nor account for. The bridge, when all is said and done, is faulty in its construction.

For whereas the poem presents itself as three stanzas running in parallel, with a last stanza that turns backs upon them all, or runs across them all, in fact we experience a notable shift between the second stanza and the third. In the first two stanzas live creatures, the birds, are transformed into machines: the swallows into crossbows, and the moor-hen into some sort of lathe. (For the double sense of "planing" is decisively tipped toward its mechanic sense, by "ripped" and "shavings.") In the third stanza, however, the kingcups are presented in normal organic terms. The shift is notable. And yet the poet gives no indication that he has noticed it. Of course, we are ready to agree with him that neither perceiving organic things as mechanical nor perceiving them as organic is as

important as the perception he has failed to make—of the human
presence, Emma's, in the room behind him. He is right to reproach
himself. But he has raised other questions which he seems to be unaware of.

Moreover, if the eye which fails to rest on Emma is the sharp
and darting eye of the technician designing his next precision job
on the basis of his finely honed perceptions, we get some sense of
what it was like to be married to a Victorian engineer (whether in
steel or in language), or to any man vowed to the Victorian ethos
of self-help. We learn what strain may be laid on human relations,
and what damage may be done to them, in an age of advanced
technology. But this is very clearly our reflection, not the poet's; a
reflection which the poem may prompt, but to which it does not
lead us. Thus this poem, like "The Wind's Prophecy," provides us
with the components for an image of Victorian technological culture, but it does not assemble those components into the image.
Where "The Wind's Prophecy" failed to provide all the components that we find we need, "Overlooking the River Stour" provides more components than it uses or takes account of.

I have two more comments to make. One is the wry confession
that years ago when I used to read this poem, I was so won over
by the brilliance of the descriptions by mechanical analogy in the
first two stanzas, that I thought: "Would that Hardy had written
thus always!" "Brilliance" is indeed the right word, but when I
was younger I did not realize that "brilliant" is double-edged; nor
did I take account of the often stated truth that vivid exactness in
descriptive images counts for nothing, unless moulded and if necessary subdued by a current of strong feeling through them. My second comment is more tentative, but may take us further. It concerns the word "honeybee'd" which, in the rhyme position, draws
attention to itself and its own audacity. It is an irregularity, in the
sense that it is an ingenious coinage not vindicated by normal usage
whether literary or spoken. But it is not one of Hardy's *cunning*
irregularities, for those by his own account he contrives in meter,
not in diction; and indeed of these frequent oddities in his diction
he seems to have been largely unaware. If so, this word is less than

masterly. It is not a seeming clumsiness, but a real one. This does not make it any better, nor is this poem any better for including it, but there *are* poems by Hardy which are redeemed by such oddities. Many critics of Hardy's poetry have found themselves in the uncomfortable and ultimately preposterous position of applauding him for his clumsiness. It may now be clear how we may be driven to such a desperate expedient: it is when we have to deal with an artist whose will is imperious, who claims by implication to be sharp-sightedly in command of every aspect of his undertakings, that we may in exceptional circumstances be grateful for the times when he shows himself fallible. For these are the times when the drilling and the riveting stop, and the eagle-eye descends from the gantry; when the civil engineer who was once a mason finds that he has to chip with his own chisel. What he does then will fall short of mechanical precision, but his artifact by its very faultiness will have something better, *virtù*, "the light of the doer as it were cleaving to it." (The words are Pound's.)

An instance springs to mind in what is often, and to my mind rightly, applauded as one of Hardy's greatest poems. This is "The Voice":

> Woman much missed, how you call to me, call to me,
> Saying that now you are not as you were
> When you had changed from the one who was all to me,
> But as at first, when our day was fair.
>
> Can it be you that I hear? Let me view you, then,
> Standing as when I drew near to the town
> Where you would wait for me: yes, as I knew you then,
> Even to the original air-blue gown!
>
> Or is it only the breeze, in its listlessness
> Travelling across the wet mead to me here,
> You being ever dissolved to existlessness,
> Heard no more again far or near?
>
> > Thus I; faltering forward,
> > Leaves around me falling,
> Wind oozing thin through the thorn from norward,
> > And the woman calling.

Many years ago F. R. Leavis remarked of "existlessness" (later it became "wan wistlessness"—there is not much to choose between the two expressions) that it "is a questionable word, a characteristic eccentricity of invention; and yet here it sounds right. The touch that there may still be about the poem of what would normally have been rustic stiffness serves as a kind of guarantee of integrity." The nature of that "guarantee" may now be clearer: the rustic stiffness guarantees integrity, only because it comes (as "a touch") in a poem which is exerting itself, and with success, to be neither rustic nor stiff but elaborately and exactly tooled. "And then," says Dr. Leavis, "there is the exquisite modulation into the last stanza." There is indeed. And the exquisiteness is registered with delight when the poem is read in isolation; but the keenness of the pleasure is heightened, and our sense of the integrity is further assured, when we consider the poem in the context of Hardy's poetry as a whole. For in that poetry it is an all but absolute rule for an intricately rigid symmetry, such as obtains between the first three stanzas, to be maintained throughout each poem. For the poet to have broken a rule he set such store by is another "guarantee of integrity." For nothing but fidelity to feeling could have caused him to do so.

Thus, in Yvor Winters's account of Hardy, one judgment that is wholly unacceptable comes, for me, when he remarks: " 'The Haunter' and 'The Voice' are companion pieces. The second has been often quoted; the first is by far the better."[11] "The Haunter" is an imperiously symmetrical piece in four eight-line stanzas, the rhyme words of the even lines in the first stanza reproduced exactly in each of the stanzas that follow. Winters does not tell us what he finds wrong with "The Voice"; in view of his preference for "The Haunter" one may suspect that he likes just that rigid symmetry which I have called technological, a symmetry which "The Voice" departs from, whereas "The Haunter" presses it home relentlessly. And sure enough, "brilliant" seems to be always for Winters a term of unqualified approval.

[11] Winters, *Forms of Discovery*, p. 192.

One critic after another complains that nearly 1000 poems are too much, and asks for a more or less agreed-upon select few, a canon on which Hardy's reputation shall rest, about which disagreements shall circle. But even on this point there are dissenting voices; Mark Van Doren's, for instance: "No poet more stubbornly resists selection. . . . There is no core of pieces, no inner set of classic or perfect poems, which would prove his rank. . . . It is the whole of him that registers and counts . . ."[12] And Philip Larkin has declared that he delights in Hardy's poems because one can have read for years up and down in the *Collected Poems,* and still be surprised by something newly discovered or previously overlooked. As the years pass, I for one find myself more and more of Van Doren's and Larkin's way of thinking. Nothing supports their case so much as the half-dozen selections of Hardy's poems that have in fact appeared; and one of them in particular, the selection made by John Crowe Ransom.[13] Ransom—what could be better? It seemed a splendidly appropriate conjunction: Ransom, the author of "Piazza Piece" and "Spectral Lovers," seemed the one poet in English since Hardy who could be relied upon to have a temperamental sympathy with Hardy's concerns and Hardy's style, and a just sense of how to discriminate between Hardy's strong poems and his weak ones. And yet, when the book appeared, among the 125 pieces printed by Ransom one looked in vain for "After a Journey," "At Castle Boterel," "The Voice," "My Spirit will not haunt the mound," "Under the Waterfall." Of "the five great elegies" which, according to another critic[14] were "the summit of Hardy's achievement," Ransom had selected just one, "The Going." And yet Ransom had not scamped his assignment. When we study his selection, and in particular his valuable introductory essay, we are forced to realize that his assessment of Hardy is not at all perfunctory. It

[12] Quoted by Howe, *Thomas Hardy,* p. 168.
[13] *Selected Poems of Thomas Hardy* (New York, 1960; in Collier Books 1966).
[14] Brown, *Thomas Hardy,* p. 176.

is not at all clear, even, that it is eccentric. And indeed, as much
must be said of the other selections that have been made by editors, or hinted at by critics. Cast about as one may, and measure
one authority against another, one perceives no consensus emerging as to what is centrally significant in Hardy's poetry, still less
therefore as to what is the canon of his secure achievements. And
if no one can determine where the center is, no one reading of the
corpus can be more eccentric than any other.

This points to something that is very important. What defeats
the attempt to discriminate the better from the worse among
Hardy's poems is not just the great number of the poems, and their
variousness. It is not even the impossibility, for the most part, of
categorizing the poems as "early" or "late"; nor the almost equal
difficulty of categorizing them according to genre, except in the
broadest and most impressionistic way. These impediments to taking Hardy the poet as a whole, the good with the bad, do not come
about by accident. Behind them is the curious paradox that Hardy,
who imposes himself so imperiously upon his medium, imposes
himself on his reader hardly at all. On every page, "Take it or
leave it," he seems to say; or, even more permissively, "Take what
you want, and leave the rest." This consciousness of having imposed on his reader so little is what lies behind Hardy's insistence
that what he offers is only a series of disconnected observations, and
behind his resentment that he should be taken as having a pessi-
mistic design upon his reader, when in fact he so sedulously
respects the reader's privilege not to be interested, not to be persuaded. It is on this basis—his respect of the reader's rights to be
attentive or inattentive as he pleases—that one rests the claim for
Hardy as perhaps the first and last "liberal" in modern poetry.
And it is because we are so unused to liberalism as a consistent attitude in a poet, that we have so much difficulty with the poetry of
Hardy.

But the outcome is that every new reader of Hardy's poetry finds
there what he wants to find. And in the event this means, for the
most part, that each reader finds in the poems what he brings to
them; what he finds there is his own pattern of preoccupations and

preferences. If this is true of every poet to some degree, of Hardy it is exceptionally true. And this is the justification for attending in particular to Ransom; since Ransom on the evidence of his own poems is an exceptionally intelligent and sophisticated reader.

What Ransom most esteems in Hardy's poetry are the poems which, after canvassing other possibilities, he finally decides to call "fables." Irving Howe, who agrees with Ransom in esteeming this kind of poem, points out:

> For having written such poems Hardy has been severely rated by critics in the Eliot line, who regard them as tritely heretical and intellectually feckless. They look with distaste upon what one of them, R. P. Blackmur, called Hardy's lack of "emotional discipline and the structural support of a received imagination" (by which immensity I take Blackmur to mean the complex of symbols and myths associated with the Christian tradition). Yet it might be remembered that we cannot always choose the situation in which we live out our lives; that for Hardy, as for many other nineteenth century writers, the loss of faith was an experience of the utmost consequence, not a mere frivolity or pretext for a wanton emotionalism; and that his effort to improvise voices, personifications and fables which might replace Christian authority was undertaken in a spirit of humility testifying not merely to the hold Christianity continued to exert upon his mind but also the depth to which its values had penetrated his very being.[15]

There is a minor puzzle here, for Ransom might well be taken as a critic "in the Eliot line," who would therefore dislike the sort of poem represented at its best by "Channel Firing" or "The Subalterns." But anyone who knows Ransom's beautiful poems can soon solve this puzzle; it was the poet in Ransom, not the critic, who wrote appreciatively of such poems:

> They offer natural images of the gods in action or, sometimes unfortunately, in inaction. The sharp and homely detail of the country naturalist in Hardy is not compromised by the presence of deity and his ministers; these are made to answer in his own language to the naturalist or his spokesman in the poem. The tone of the composition may be altogether grave and earnest. But fable is

15 Howe, *Thomas Hardy*, p. 175.

a self-confessed fiction by an independent thinker, therefore very
free in its images. As if to allow in advance for the failure of human speculations, including his own, Hardy often gives them a
sporting or rowdy turn which makes them comic in their irony.[16]

"A sporting or rowdy turn . . ." Well, this is forcing the note a
little. It is true that in "Channel Firing" the dead Parson Thirdly
is made to say, "I wish I had stuck to pipes and beer." But this is
not the note that Hardy's poem ends on; whereas Ransom's poem
"Armageddon" does indeed come to rest on lines which are "comic
in their irony":

> The immortal Adversary shook his head:
> If now they fought too long, then he would famish;
> And if much blood was shed, why, he was squeamish.
> "These Armageddons weary me much," he said.

All the same, "Armageddon" is, like other fine poems by Ransom,
Hardyesque. And we must agree that Hardy's sense of humor is
not asleep even in "The Subalterns":

> I
> "Poor wanderer," said the leaden sky,
>   "I fain would lighten thee,
> But there are laws in force on high
>   Which say it must not be."
>
> II
> "—I would not freeze thee, shorn one," cried
>   The North, "knew I but how
> To warm my breath, to slack my stride,
>   But I am ruled as thou."
>
> III
> "—Tomorrow I attack thee, wight,"
>   Said Sickness. "Yet I swear
> I bear thy little ark no spite
>   But am bid enter there."
>
> IV
> "—Come hither, Son," I heard Death say;
>   "I did not will a grave

[16] Ransom, *Selected Poems of Thomas Hardy*, p. x.

> Should end thy pilgrimage today,
> But I too am a slave."

v

> We smiled upon each other then,
> And life to me had less
> Of that fell look it wore ere when
> They owned their passiveness.

Ransom's account of this poem is scrupulous, exhaustive, and compelling. He notes for instance the firm symmetry by which each of the subalterns except the first employs a figure out of the traditional rhetoric of Christian devotion—the shorn lamb, the ark, the pilgrim; and yet he sees that this and other symmetries are those of the mason, not the engineer:

> The ecclesiastical architect in Hardy must have liked to find the poem looking this way; he would have been familiar with the series of members precisely equal in weight and function, yet different individually, in a good structure of masonry.[17]

We think of masonry rather than engineering because here both meter and rhyme are by Hardy's standards, sober; and so the mastery can manage symmetries of both without advertising itself as "brilliant." It is noteworthy and regrettable that "The Subalterns" does not appear among the 175 poems chosen by W. E. Williams for his "Thomas Hardy" in the Penguin Poets.

On the other hand, once we have admitted "Channel Firing" and "The Subalterns" as fine achievements in this kind, it is not clear from either Ransom or Howe what others we should set beside them. Irving Howe indeed cites two examples of failure in this kind: "The Masked Face" and "New Year's Eve." The latter poem is printed by both Williams and Ransom, though by Ransom it is unaccountably deprived of its last three stanzas. It is very unattractive, doubtless (as Howe suggests) because the intellectual difficulty which provoked it has not fired the poet to any "remembered or imagined situation which serves him as an emblem of the diffi-

[17] Ransom, *Selected Poems of Thomas Hardy*, p. xiv.

culty." As Howe says, "Despite the dogmas of certain critics, a poetry of statement can be written, and written well: but not by Hardy." From time to time such poetry, turning on the same intellectual difficulties as troubled Hardy and out of a mood very like Hardy's in "New Year's Eve," was written by the author of A *Shropshire Lad*; and in fact a poem like "New Year's Eve" challenges, and fails to sustain, comparison with Housman.

Indeed Housman it is who comes insistently to mind when Ransom declares: "Hardy the poet rates for us as decidedly the principal Voice of Irony among the poets of his age." Housman surely merits that description far more than Hardy. Only in his weaker poems, like "New Year's Eve," is Hardy content to settle for irony. And indeed Ransom delivers himself of this judgment on Hardy at precisely the time when he is chiding him for not letting Irony have the last word, but reserving it for "the Spirit of Pity." This happens in the fable poem, "And There Was a Great Calm," on which Ransom's comments are very odd indeed. Can "one of the noble war poems in our language, or any language," afford such lines as these?

> The feeble folk at home had grown full-used
> To "dug-outs," "snipers," "Huns," from the war-adept
> In the mornings heard, and at evetides perused;
> To day-dreamt men in millions, when they mused—
> To nightmare-men in millions when they slept.

("Day-dreamt" for "day-dreaming" is surely inexcusable.) But it appears that Ransom praises the poem in general thus extravagantly, only so as to object in particular that "Hardy is constitutionally so much under the domination of Pity, and so close to the event when he writes the Armistice poem, that he disparages the tone of the Spirit of Irony," and so fails "to represent a great Spirit according to his honors." And so we realize what was involved for Ransom when he insisted that Hardy often gave his speculations "a sporting or rowdy turn which makes them comic in their irony." This is what Ransom does himself in a poem like "Armageddon"; and what he wants to do is to take over Hardy's

irony while dispensing with Hardy's pity. Accordingly, he in-
geniously over-reads the last stanza of "Channel Firing," so as to
find an irony where I think there is none.[18] If irony matters so
much to Ransom he ought to prefer Housman to Hardy; but we
may take it he knows very well the price he would have to pay
for that exchange, how much there is in Hardy that we have to
agree not to ask Housman for, how much of variety and tangible
particularity must be given up for the sake of Housman's irony. (A
better fable poem, incidentally, is one provoked by the Boer War,
"The Souls of the Slain," which has the same setting as Housman's
"The Isle of Portland.")

Since the First World War, through and since the Great De-
pression until the day before yesterday, an ironical stance before
experience has been much favored and highly extolled in literature
by various sorts of humanist, including those sorts that call themselves, or may be called, "tragic," or even "Christian." But to the
scientific humanist, who pins his faith as Hardy did on "loving-
kindness operating through scientific knowledge," irony can never
have more than a subordinate place in the moral economy. And
indeed in those words Hardy declared that for him the Spirit of
Pity, not Irony, would always have the last word. Moreover, the
irony of Hardy and Housman alike is in any case quite different
from most modern irony; the older poets do not recommend
irony as a secure or dignified stance from which to confront reality,
rather it is the stance of reality as it confronts *us*. Their irony is
cosmic, where an Auden's is provisional and strategic. Armored in
irony, the liberal may be, though ineffective, invulnerable; but
Hardy's poems open a window on a world where liberalism may yet
be a passion—as, one likes to believe, it always has been in the
laboratories.

A comparison of Hardy with Housman may be taken a stage
further. For when a reader so scrupulous and sensitive as Ransom
reads a poem askew, it's likely we have to do with a sort of mis-
reading that will be persistent unless we can scotch it. We may

[18] Ransom, *Selected Poems of Thomas Hardy*, p. xii.

consider, then, a poem by Housman and a poem by Hardy which
offer themselves for comparison for an unusually good reason, in
that each of them is clearly a variation on a classic poem by Wordsworth, the eight-line masterpiece, "A Slumber Did My Spirit Seal."
Here is the Housman:

> The night is freezing fast,
>   Tomorrow comes December;
>   And winterfalls of old
> Are with me from the past;
>   And chiefly I remember
>   How Dick would hate the cold.
>
> Fall, winter, fall; for he,
>   Prompt hand and headpiece clever,
>   Has woven a winter robe,
> And made of earth and sea
>   His overcoat for ever,
>   And wears the turning globe.[19]

Hardy's poem is called, "While Drawing in a Churchyard":

> "It is sad that so many of worth,
>   Still in the flesh," soughed the yew,
> "Misjudge their lot whom kindly earth
>   Secludes from view.
>
> "They ride their diurnal round
> Each day-span's sum of hours
> In peerless ease, without jolt or bound
>   Or ache like ours.
>
> "If the living could but hear
> What is heard by my roots as they creep
> Round the restful flock, and the things said there
>   No one would weep."
>
> " 'Now set among the wise,'
> They say: 'Enlarged in scope,
> That no God trumpet us to rise
>   We truly hope.' "

[19] A. E. Housman, *Last Poems* (London, 1922), xx, p. 43.

I listened to his strange tale
In the mood that stillness brings,
And I grew to accept as the day wore pale
That show of things.

Ransom or anyone else could readily explicate the irony in "show" in Hardy's last line. But the "sporting or rowdy turn" is all Housman's, in his veering from "robe" to "overcoat." The irony is what Housman is working for, and attains; when we have taken the force of it, we have taken the force of Housman's poem. In Hardy, the irony is acknowledged and allowed for; and yet, for all that the irony comes in the last line, the total response worked for and earned by Hardy, though it thus incorporates irony, goes beyond it or envelops it. It is only when we rate the ironical vision less highly than Ransom does, that we appreciate the human breadth of Hardy's feeling, and how far—on this showing at least—he transcends Housman.

All the same, this comparison prompts other reflections. John Wain, comparing Housman's poem unsympathetically with its Wordsworth model, complains that "the over-artful stanza form seems vulgar by comparison."[20] And this may be true. But metrically, of course, Housman's stanza is quite straightforward, and its intricate look on the page is merely a typographical device for showing how it is structured according to rhyme; it is Hardy's stanza that is artful *metrically*. And is it not true that by the side of the Wordsworth original (which Hardy must have had in mind no less than Housman—the word "diurnal" says as much), it is Hardy's stanza that seems *over*-artful? Formally, Hardy's little poem is ambitious; inwardly or humanly, though Hardy's poem is more ambitious than Housman's, it falls almost as short as that does of the masterly succinctness of "A Slumber Did My Spirit Seal."

And this is a crucial point. A great deal of the trouble we have with Hardy come of our wanting to consider as an ambitious poet

[20] John Wain, "Housman," in *Preliminary Essays* (London, 1957); reprinted in *A. E. Housman: A Collection of Critical Essays*, ed. by Christopher Ricks (Englewood Cliffs, N.J., 1968), p. 31.

like Wordsworth a poet who was very unambitious indeed, as we
know from external as well as internal evidence. If we read "While
Drawing in a Churchyard" as a relaxed and leisurely though
formally adroit gloss on a great poem by Wordsworth, it may be
that this is as much as the poet hoped for. As with other sorts of
poem by Hardy, so with these verse fables, we are in no time at
all looking at poems which are "all right in their way" or "very
good of their kind"—poems like "God-forgotten," "By the
Earth's Corpse," "To the Unknown God" and "God's Education."
Hardy was very ambitious technically, and unambitious every other
way—like, once again, the Victorian architect, who knew he could
construct an Early English chancel more elaborately exact than
the thirteenth century could manage, but didn't (unless he was
stupid) suppose that he had thereby recovered the spirituality of
the Age of Faith. The implications of this are far-reaching for the
poets who come after Hardy and take him as their model or their
master.

For what we are saying is that, except in the ill-starred and pre-
mature *Dynasts*, Hardy the poet comes before us as "the honest
journeyman," highly skilled indeed but disablingly modest in his
aims. We reached this recognition as soon as we noticed how little
Hardy imposes himself on his reader. On page after page he bows
and retires at just the point where another poet would, for good or
ill, advance and take us by the throat. At first we are so disconcerted that we cannot believe our eyes or our ears; then we are won
over by such unaccustomed civility. And yet we remain disconcerted, because so completely disarmed. (The effect is not created
by any quality of Hardy's conception or of his images, but by his
formal disposition of verse lines; his symmetrical stanzas lie on the
page demurely self-contained.)

Very much to the point here are the many poems by Hardy
which may be called "occasional." The honest journeyman rises
dutifully to public occasions, like an unofficial poet laureate. Witness his "Poems of the Past and Present," where a loyal homage to
Queen Victoria lately dead introduces a dozen poems on the Boer
War. These include "Drummer Hodge," and we realize how dis-
arming Hardy is when we see this poem esteemed by some who

would castigate Rupert Brooke's "1914," though the senselessness of war is glossed over by the same means in the one poem as in the other. Similarly, though John Crowe Ransom was right to reprove the reader who thought "Channel Firing" was mere saber-rattling, it is disingenuous to remember this poem and "In Time of 'The Breaking of Nations,'" while forgetting several other poems by Hardy that are indeed saber-rattlings or morale-builders or worse.

Yet the Boer War sequence included "The Souls of the Slain," which is important and memorable. And in fact Hardy scored some of his most notable successes with occasional poems. R. P. Blackmur notes some of these:

> such poems as those (sic) about the loss of the *Titanic*, with its extraordinary coiling imagery . . . such poems as those on Leslie Stephen and Swinburne, each ending with a magnificently appropriate image, Stephen being joined to the Schreckhorn which he had scaled, and Swinburne joined with the waves—
>
> > Him once their peer in sad improvisations,
> > And deft as wind to cleave their frothy manes—
>
> and again such poems as "Channel Firing" and "In Time of 'The Breaking of Nations,'" which need no comment; and finally in such poems as "An Ancient to Ancients" with its dignity and elegance making the strength of old age. But these poems are or ought to be too generally received to permit their being looked at as anything except isolated, like something in the Oxford Book of English Verse.[21]

Here Blackmur begins with occasional poems and ends with anthology pieces—"like something in the Oxford Book of English Verse." And I think this is right; for the same "honest journeyman" attitude lies behind both sorts of poem. And indeed the two sorts of poem are really one. Consider "The Darkling Thrush." This is the poem with which, in *The Times* at New Year 1900, Hardy greeted the new century. But surely it is also contrived so as to earn just the fate which has come upon it—of being in all the anthologies.

I do not know that any one has defined the term "anthology

---

[21] R. P. Blackmur, "The Shorter Poems of Thomas Hardy," in *Language as Gesture* (London, 1954), p. 75.

piece," or explained and justified the disparaging inflection which
hangs about it. If we remember "The Lake Isle of Innisfree" as
Yeats's anthology piece, and recall how bitterly Yeats came to re-
sent its notoriety, we may approach a definition: an anthology piece
is a poem which, whether by luck or design, and whatever its other
virtues, cannot give offence. "The Darkling Thrush" answers to
this description, as does (I'm afraid) that other favorite of the
anthologists, "The Oxen." And who can think that the innocu-
ousness of "The Darkling Thrush" on New Year's Day 1900 was
arrived at by luck, by being for instance luckily abstracted from a
context which would have cast a guilty shadow on its innocence?
A modern enthusiast for the poem, John Berryman,[22] makes much
of the irony latent in the last line:

> Some blessèd Hope, whereof he knew
> And I was unaware.

(That is to say, the hope is an illusion.) But can we doubt that
the reader of *The Times* in 1900, and the readers of the anthologies ever since and at present, read the lines quite differently, to
mean: "I, the notorious pessimist and author of *Jude the Obscure*,
humbly confess myself foolish beside the sanguine and resolute
wisdom of this bird"? And—a nastier question—can we doubt
that Hardy, either when he wrote the poem for this occasion or else
when he mailed it to *The Times* to meet the occasion, counted
upon the editor and the regular readers of the newspaper to take it
in just that up-beat, unexpectionable way? Such are the dishonest-
ies, or the opportunities for dishonesty, which attend a poet who,
like Hardy, declares that his highest ambition is to place one or
two poems in an anthology like *The Golden Treasury*.

We must not be unfair. We have every reason to believe that
Hardy's respect for Queen Victoria, and for a Victorian institution
like Palgrave's *Golden Treasury*, was sincere. There is no reason
to think that Hardy had misgivings about his country and his nation, which he ignobly stifled. Quite the contrary indeed. A techni-

---

[22] John Berryman, in *Master Poems of the English Language*, ed. Oscar Williams (New York, 1966), pp. 788-90.

cian such as Hardy was, and conceived himself to be, needs to believe that decisions are being wisely taken elsewhere about what
the ventures are to which his technical expertise shall be applied.
Others decide whether the railway bridge is necessary; the engineer
is responsible only for building it safely, elegantly, strongly. Major
issues of national policy were among the matters that Hardy was
too modest to concern himself with; and his modesty was that of
the expert technician, imperious within his expertise, diffident or
indifferent outside it.

Accordingly, in most of the senses of "great" as we apply it to
poets, Hardy is not a great poet at all. He is not "great" because,
except in *The Dynasts*, he does not choose to be, does not enter
himself in that competition. This is the burden of R. P. Blackmur's
essay of 1940, "The Shorter Poems of Thomas Hardy." Blackmur
insists that, tot up as we may the sum of admirable poems by
Hardy, what stops him short of greatness is something in the quality of his attention to experience and to the poetic rendering of it.
It is not a matter of his having only so many admirable poems to
plead his case for him, but of something that is built into his
poems even at their most admirable. If we say that even at his best
Hardy was not enough the craftsman, we certainly do not mean
what Yeats meant when he said (incredibly) that Hardy's work
"lacked technical accomplishment."[23] (In sheer *accomplishment*,
especially of prosody, Hardy beats Yeats hands down.) We mean
that Hardy failed to be a craftsman to just the degree that he insisted on being the triumphant technician. As Blackmur put it,
"what Hardy really lacked was the craft of his profession—technique in the wide sense." Hardy too often lacked craft, to just the
extent that he had expertise; he lacked technique "in the wide
sense," to just the degree that he exulted in possessing it in its
narrower senses. The honesty of the honest journeyman may be
dishonest in his master.

It may not be clear how Hardy the technician is related to Hardy
the scientific humanist and Hardy the "liberal." But the relation is

[23] W. B. Yeats, Introduction to *The Oxford Book of Modern Verse* (London,
1937), p. xiv.

one that is familiar enough, though we seldom encounter it, or any analogue of it, in poetry. It is the relation between pure science and applied science, a crucial relation for any advanced technological culture, and one which throws up in many aspects of that culture—for instance, in its politics—precisely the contradiction that I am struggling to define in Hardy's attitude to his art, and his practice of it. For we accuse the corporate enterprise of science and technology of being insufferably and perilously arrogant in the way that it manipulates and conditions us and our environment. And yet the individual scientist or engineer often sees himself, quite sincerely, as very modest, merely an honest worker at specific tasks and problems. It is not he, but the literary man or the philosopher, who has the presumption to question the whole cultural design, and offer to set the whole world to rights! In just the same way the liberal in politics usually contends that he addresses himself to each question "on its merits"; and he rejects as intolerably presumptuous the radical's contention that each and every question—for instance, whether a university should harbor an officers' training corps—must be related to the ultimate issues of how, if at all, mankind is to survive on this planet. At the scientist in his laboratory, as at the earnest liberal in his committee, the radical throws the angry word "cop-out"—meaning by that precisely that the individual's modesty is what makes possible the corporate presumption. And Hardy in his poetry is this sort of cop-out, a modest (though proudly expert) workman in a corporate enterprise which from time to time publishes a balance-sheet called *The Golden Treasury* or *The Oxford Book of English Verse*.

These are harsh words, but it may be that harshness is what is called for. For it begins to look as if Hardy's engaging modesty and his decent liberalism represent a crucial selling short of the poetic vocation, for himself and his successors. For surely the poet, if any one, has a duty to be radical, to go to the roots. So much at least all poets have assumed through the centuries. Hardy, perhaps without knowing it, questions that assumption, and appears to reject it. Some of his successors in England, and a few out of England, seem to have agreed with him.

~2~
Hardy
Self-Excelling

In five-score summers! All new eyes,
New minds, new modes, new fools, new wise;
New woes to weep, new joys to prize;

With nothing left of me and you
In that live century's vivid view
Beyond a pinch of dust or two;

A century which, if not sublime,
Will show, I doubt not, at its prime,
A scope above this blinkered time.

—Yet what to me how far above?
For I would only ask thereof
That thy worm should be my worm, Love![1]

But does not Hardy quite often excel himself, and escape from the limitations which we have gracelessly insisted upon, and labored, through the last chapter? Indeed he does. Time and again he writes in ways that it seems his declared intentions and his professed ideology would have ruled out.

To be sure, there are certain ranges of poetic fiction which he will never stray into. For instance, when he wrote scornfully in 1922 how "belief in witches of Endor is displacing the Darwinian theory," must we not believe that among those "witches of Endor"

[1] Thomas Hardy, "1967." The poem was written in 1867.

Hardy would have included mythological ladies like Demeter and Artemis? And if so, there can be no doubt of his impatience with a declaration by one of his younger contemporaries, Ezra Pound:

> Speaking aesthetically, the myths are explications of mood: you may stop there, or you may probe deeper. Certain it is that these myths are only intelligible in a vivid and glittering sense to those people to whom they occur. I know, I mean, one man who understands Persephone and Demeter, and one who understands the Laurel, and another who has, I should say, met Artemis. These things are for them *real*.[2]

Hardy would surely have responded to this very much as would his disciple Philip Larkin, who thirty years later in a strident phrase which has become famous, impatiently declared his disbelief in "a common myth-kitty." It is easy to share their impatience when Pound strikes into this way of talking, as he does (to give another example) in his essay of 1915, "Arnold Dolmetsch":

> The first myths arose when a man walked sheer into "nonsense," that is to say, when some very vivid and undeniable adventure befell him, and he told someone else who called him a liar. Thereupon, after bitter experience, perceiving that no one could understand what he meant when he said that he "turned into a tree," he made a myth—a work of art that is—an impersonal or objective story woven out of his own emotion, as the nearest equation that he was capable of putting into words. That story, perhaps, then gave rise to a weaker copy of his emotion in others, until there arose a cult, a company of people who could understand each other's nonsense about the gods.

But then, writing about Pound would be a great deal more responsible, and hostile readers like Philip Larkin would get the attention they deserve, if critics, when they quote passages like these, would pause long enough to say explicitly whether from their own experience they know what it means to "meet Artemis," to "turn

[2] Pound, "Psychology and Troubadours" (1916), reprinted as Chapter V of *The Spirit of Romance* (New York reprint 1968), p. 92.

into a tree," to "walk sheer into nonsense." I will confess at once that my own experience provides me with not an inkling of what these expressions mean.

And accordingly I owe it to myself to refuse the trust which I am asked to give, that for other persons "these things are . . . real." Does this seem very illiberal? Or is it not the merest prudence, and of a firmly liberal kind, to refuse, without supporting evidence from one's own experience, the claim of others to have private revelations of a supra-rational sort? After all, on the basis of such revelations, do we not hear it contended that the Elders of Zion have planned world conquest; that black and brown peoples must be servants of the whites; that peasants and artisans are happy in Mao's China; that the German nation is called to rule over Europe, the Japanese over Asia. . . ? In short, who is to persuade me—and how—that the man who says he has met Artemis or turned into a tree is not dangerously self-deluded or self-intoxicated? And is not this in fact the central and unavoidable question about Pound's poetry, as about Charles Olson's and Robert Duncan's? One would not think so, scanning the many pages of criticism already devoted to these poets. It would certainly have been the question raised by Hardy.

However, in Pound's theory and practice there is a range of supra-rational apprehensions which falls short of the take-it-or-leave-it of "he turned into a tree." Pound writes, for instance, in his essay, "Mediaevalism":

The Tuscan demands harmony in something more than the plastic. He declines to limit his aesthetic to the impact of light on the eye . . . This really complicates the aesthetic. You deal with an interactive force: the *virtù* in short.

And dealing with it is not anti-life. It is not maiming, it is not curtailment. The senses at first seem to project for a few yards beyond the body. Effect of a decent climate where a man leaves his nerve-set open, or allows it to tune into its ambience . . . The conception of the body as perfect instrument of the increasing intelligence pervades.

And this is immediately related to a crucial passage, later in the same ambitious essay, which is quoted, and rightly, by every commentator. It comes where Pound is characterizing the lost world of Cavalcanti, a world which Cavalcanti's poems take for granted:

> the radiant world where one thought cuts through another with clean edge, a world of moving energies *"mezzo oscuro rade,"* *"risplende in se perpetuale effecto,"* magnetisms that take form, that are seen, or that border the visible, the matter of Dante's *paradiso*, the glass under water, the form that seems a form seen in a mirror, these realities perceptible to the sense, interacting . . . this "harmony in the sentience" or harmony of the sentient, where the thought has its demarcation. . . .

Are there people, poets indeed and readers of poetry, to whom "one thought cuts through another with clean edge," and "a man leaves his nerve-set open," and "the thought has its demarcation," are propositions as meaningless—as little corroborated by personal experience—as is for others the statement, "He met Artemis"? My experience suggests that there are people thus disadvantaged. And, without taking too seriously Pound's reference to "a decent climate" (for we may suspect that the perceptions described are more common among Nordic travelers to Italy, than among Italians), still we may believe that people to whom both sets of propositions seem meaningless are often English.

English or not, what are such readers to do, in all honesty and the merest prudence? Finding that "one thought cuts through another with clean edge" is (after self-scrutiny and some patient exercise) meaningless to them, must they not declare that this range or level of the poet's experience is as closed to them, and just as suspect, as the mythological level is closed and suspect to others? I believe they must, and do; though they need to notice, as they seldom do, that they thereby declare themselves shut out not just from much of Pound's poetry, nor just from a Poundian though English poet such as Basil Bunting or Charles Tomlinson, nor from an Italianized one like Rossetti, but also from English poets thought of as thoroughly insular. The last stanza of Philip Larkin's

"The Whitsun Weddings" is, or ought to be, equally meaningless to a reader who does not know from experience how thoughts can be "magnetisms that take form, that are seen, or that border the visible." And those last phrases from Pound seem to be the very stuff of "After a Journey," by Larkin's master, Hardy:

> Hereto I come to view a voiceless ghost;
>   Whither, O whither will its whim now draw me?
> Up the cliff, down, till I'm lonely, lost,
>   And the unseen waters' ejaculations awe me.
> Where you will next be there's no knowing,
>   Facing round about me everywhere,
>   With your nut-coloured hair,
> And gray eyes, and rose-flush coming and going.

The status of Hardy's ghosts is very hard to determine. On the one hand, they seem to be merely Virgilian stage properties, in Hardy as in his contemporary and friend Masefield. But Masefield does not come before us as an atheistic humanist, as Hardy does; and in any case some of Hardy's ghosts are more "real" than others, as we shall see. Hardy is disingenuous; we encounter in his poems things that are not dreamed of in his philosophy. And this is troublesome. But of course we must trust the poem, not the poet.

If, still with Hardy in mind, we range Ezra Pound's poems and perceptions on a scale of diminishing complexity and increasing accessibility, we find other levels of poetic experience treated by Pound, each of them less exacting than either the mythological or the level we have just been discussing. We find, that is to say, the experiences comprised within, or lying on the frontiers of, Imagism.

Even with Imagism the English reader has had great difficulties, and has them still, being by no means helped by seemingly willful darkenings of counsel on the part of some whom he had every right to take as authorities—influential academic critics in England who have used "imagism" as a blanket term to cover all developments in Anglo-American poetry since French *symbolisme* made its impact, or else as merely an Anglo-American variant on Sym-

bolist doctrine and practice. There is an amusing irony here because, as Schniedau and others have hinted,[3] the influential figure
behind at any rate Pound's imagism is the Englishman, Ford
Madox Ford (whom, to be sure, the English for the most part
refuse to read); and moreover—a very nice point which I think is
original with Schniedau—the characteristic and much prized terseness of the Imagist poem seems to owe something to the laconic
understatement of the English upper classes, a linguistic or rhetorical phenomenon which fascinated the Americans among the
original Imagists.

Pound, it will be recalled, speculated that a myth came into being when a man who had "turned into a tree," despairing of finding a hearer for direct narration of this experience, made instead
"an impersonal or objective story woven out of his own emotion,
as the nearest equation that he was capable of putting into words."
This mathematical analogue—the "equation"—was used by Pound
in other contexts, and sometimes he elaborated the analogy into
specific parallels between poetry and algebra (much as, across the
Channel, Valéry was doing, and was to do, in explaining to himself
the procedures of Mallarmé). Schniedau makes it clear that for
Pound this was a great deal more than just a modish flourish. As
used by Pound, this algebraic analogue puts at the center of
Imagist aesthetic the device of the *synecdoche*, the part that stands
for the whole (in happy cases, the particular that stands for the
universal). Indeed this marks the point at which, in Pound's most
considered thinking about Imagism, he goes beyond his mentor
Ford, and raises Ford's novelistic impressionism to the power and
tension of poetry. What Pound learned from Ford (not without
pain, for it involved abandoning his own earlier styles as well as
much instruction from his other mentor, Yeats) was the superiority
to mere "description" of that "presentation" which Pound and
Ford alike associated above all with Stendhal or Flaubert. The
"equation," sparer and more demanding of the reader even than
"presentation," represents a tightening of the screw beyond Ford's

[3] Herbert Schniedau, *Ezra Pound: The Image and the Real* (Baton Rouge,
1969).

stories and poems. Thus Imagism strictly speaking is concerned with *equations* for emotional experience, not presentations of it through images, still less implications or evocations of it through cumulative description of attendant physical properties.

This argument supplies us with three further levels of poetic artifice, in descending order of exactingness—equation, presentation, description. And Hardy exerted himself on all three levels. Here, for instance, is what I take to be an Imagist equation, "Snow in the Suburbs":

> Every branch big with it,
> Bent every twig with it;
> Every fork like a white web-foot;
> Every street and pavement mute:
> Some flakes have lost their way, and grope back upward, when
> Meeting those meandering down they turn and descend again.
> The palings are glued together like a wall,
> And there is no waft of wind with the fleecy fall.
>
> A sparrow enters the tree
> Whereon immediately
> A snow-lump thrice his own slight size
> Descends on him and showers his head and eyes,
> And overturns him,
> And near inurns him,
> And lights on a nether twig, when its brush
> Starts off a volley of other lodging lumps with a rush.
>
> The steps are a blanched slope,
> Up which, with feeble hope,
> A black cat comes, wide-eyed and thin;
> And we take him in.

And here is a "presentation," "A Spellbound Palace" (subtitled "Hampton Court"):

> On this kindly yellow day of mild low-travelling winter sun
> The stirless depth of the yews
> Are vague with misty blues:
> Across the spacious pathways stretching spires of shadow
> run,
> And the wind-gnawed walls of ancient brick are fired
> vermilion.

Two or three early sanguine finches tune
Some tentative strains, to be enlarged by May or June:
From a thrush or blackbird
Comes now and then a word,
While an enfeebled fountain somewhere within is heard.

Our footsteps wait awhile,
Then draw beneath the pile,
When an inner court outspreads
As 'twere History's own asile,
Where the now-visioned fountain its attenuate crystal sheds
In passive lapse that seems to ignore the yon world's clamorous
clutch,
And lays an insistent numbness on the place, like a cold hand's
touch.

And there swaggers the Shade of a straddling King, plumed,
sworded, with sensual face,
And lo, too, that of his Minister, at a bold self-centred pace:
Sheer in the sun they pass; and thereupon all is still,
Save the mindless fountain tinkling on with thin enfeebled will.

(Ghosts are frequent denizens of Hardy's poems; but these shades
of Henry VIII and Wolsey are, in no derogatory sense, conventional, as the woman's ghost in "After a Journey" certainly is not.)
As for a poem by Hardy that is brilliantly descriptive, no more,
we have looked at one such already, "Overlooking the River
Stour," a poem which itself confesses, guiltily, that its composition
did not engage the full attention of its author. It thus proclaims
its own minor or marginal status; and yet of course, so long as
description is so vividly exact and inventive as in that poem, we
cannot wish to deny to description a place, if perhaps a humble
one, within the legitimate endeavors and performances that we
call poetry. A rung or many rungs beneath description, and beneath the dignity of poetry, is inert observation (however accurate) and enumeration, such as are found allegedly in a young
British poet perhaps unfairly parodied:[4]

---

[4] *Expostulations*, by Teddy Hogge, and *The Wooden Muse*, Part One, by
Alec Pope (London, 1970), p. 13.

Down in Rowntree Road
Motorbikes, dogshit and girls
Are words, words, words,
Not *motorbikes, dogshit* and *girls* . . .

When thou hast Dunn
Thou hast not done,
For he has more
Words like motorbikes, dogshit, girls.

My point is to suggest that the now fivefold scale, from description through presentation to equation, and thence through the
ghostly to myth—a scale perhaps of mounting intensity, certainly
of increasing scope and ambitiousness—is one upon which to place
quite a lot of poems by Hardy. Of course, the distinctions within
it are not clear-cut; and it may raise problems that are sterile because mechanical. For instance *The Dynasts* is offered rather
plainly as "myth"; if it fails to satisfy on that level, does it—or can
it—earn our esteem on some other? (I would guess not.)

No distinction is more crucial than that between presentation
and Imagist equation. Pasternak wrote, in 1922:

> People nowadays imagine that art is like a fountain, whereas it is
> a sponge. They think art has to flow forth, whereas what it has to
> do is absorb and become saturated. They suppose that it can be
> divided up into means of depiction, whereas it is made up of the
> organs of perception.[5]

An English critic, Martin Dodsworth, noting this declaration, was
disconcerted to come across poems by Pasternak where a quality
of sparseness, even meagerness, in the scene which the poem renders is registered appreciatively or at least without reprobation.[6]
But Pasternak seems to have been as much of an Imagist as Pound
was, at least in the sense that he sought to give not presentations
of experience, still less descriptions, but equations for it. And in

[5] Pasternak, Neskol'ko polozhenii (1922); see *Sochineniya* [*Works*] (Ann
Arbor, 1961), III, 152.
[6] Martin Dodsworth, in *The Review*, No. 22 (June 1970), pp. 46-47.

poetry as in mathematics an equation is above all economical, elegantly spare. The Imagist poem, like the short poems of Pasternak, epitomizes experience by anatomizing it; as Schniedau says, it is characteristic of the Imagist poem to be skeletal. The Pasternakian "saturation" in no way denies this; at the cost of mixing metaphors let us say that only when the poet is saturated with an experience is he in a position to anatomize it, to distill from it not a description nor even a presentation but an anatomy, an equation. (When Wordsworth speaks of "emotion recollected in tranquillity," the "tranquillity" stands for the saturation, the "recollecting" for the distillation.)

And in fact Pasternak is very Poundian indeed, but very Hardy-esque also, when he opts for poetry as sponge, not as fountain. Poets and students of poetry do not need phenomenologists to tell them that any successful encounter between subject and object, certainly any such encounter that is at once fine enough and resonant enough to germinate a poem, has to be marked above all by reciprocity, by a giving that is equal (and no more than equal) to a taking. But, that once said, it makes a difference from which point of view we regard the transaction, from the point of view of the subject or of the object; in short, which way the traffic is run, from inside out or from outside in. And Pasternak's figure of the sponge ranges him firmly with Pound, with Williams, with George Oppen—in fact with the whole Imagist and post-Imagist tradition in American poetry, which envisages the traffic run from outside in, not the other way around. It is probably as true now as it was in 1922 that "people nowadays imagine art is like a fountain." Doubtless, even in a freed Russia, Blok and Mayakovsky would be more popular than Pasternak; just as on both sides of the Atlantic, Ginsberg and Lowell are, and will continue to be, more popular than George Oppen and Charles Tomlinson. For readers, it seems, will always take more readily to the subjective making demands on the objective, than to any traffic the other way. And for this reason most readers, even in England, will always find Hardy's poetry, however estimable and touching, insufficiently exciting. For Hardy, though he seems to have lived through the Imagist Movement and its immediate aftermath without being aware of them, is certainly among those who see poetry as sponge rather than fountain—as both "Snow in the Suburbs" and "A Spellbound Palace" should have shown.

In something like the lyric sequence "Razryv" ("The Break"), as in many other places, Pasternak can be seen to have moved beyond Imagist anatomizing.[7] And Hardy moves there also; as I have contended, the author of "Wessex Heights" was one of those "certain men" who, as Pound said, "move in phantasmagoria; the images of their gods, whole countrysides, stretches of hill and forest travel with them":

> There's a ghost at Yell'ham Bottom chiding loud at the fall of
> the night,
> There's a ghost in Froom-side Vale, thin-lipped and vague, in
> a shroud of white,
> There is one in the railway train whenever I do not want it
> near,
> I see its profile against the pane, saying what I would not hear.

Hardy's "gods" are always ghosts; but certainly as he travels, whole countrysides travel with him. Of poem after poem by Hardy, as of story after story, we can say that what occasions them is topog-

---

[7] It is also true that in some poems Pasternak moves on or up to that level of *myth*, where as I have confessed I cannot follow him nor Pound nor any poet —the level on which Pound is able to say, in his obituary of Ford, "he saw quite distinctly the Venus immortal crossing the tram tracks." Since I have followed Herbert Schniedau gratefully in a great deal, I ought to make it clear that this is where I depart from him. The point may be crucial. For it's on the assumption that "myth" is the central business of the *Cantos* that Schniedau rests his ingenious case that the *Cantos*, being essentially a compendium of myths like Ovid's *Metamorphoses*, had to deny themselves that "unity of surface" which Pound once found "boring" in Pope, Racine, Corneille. What we are offered instead is that current shibboleth, "composition by field." The argument, however, is unsound; for in one of its aspects Pope's *Dunciad*, for all its "unity of surface," *is* a compendium of myth, as Aubrey Williams and others have shown. True to my predilections or my limitations, I esteem that dimension of Pope's masterpiece much less than its magnificently sustained and curious phantasmagoria.

raphy, a reality of place rather than time. Carl Weber has worked
out that the cycle of the Wessex novels and stories is devised in
such a way as to span, decade by decade, the course of the nineteenth century through that area of southwest England. But of
course what most insistently strikes the reader of Hardy's prose is
not this charting of historical time, but a mapping of physical space.
What the reader of Hardy first needs—and this is as true of the
poems as of the stories—is not a history of nineteenth-century
England, but a map. Significant is the presence of poems entitled
"In Front of the Landscape" and "The Place on the Map." Time
brings in its revenges, and now that Edwin Muir in Britain has
despairingly protested, "Nothing can come of history but history,"
now that in the United States, Charles Olson and other poets have
set themselves to learn from geographers like Herodotus and C. O.
Sauer and J. Tuzo Wilson,[8] it should be easier to understand how
and why, in the poems of bereavement after the death of his first
wife, Hardy's imagination turned continually on the difference
between her native Cornwall and the Dorset he took her to, where
she lies buried. It will be noticed, with newly heightened sympathy, how in his poems for Leslie Stephen and Swinburne, Hardy
identified both men with patches of physical space which in their
lives they attached themselves to—in Swinburne's case, the Channel coast, in Stephen's the Alpine peak of the Schreckhorn. And
it will be noticed too that location matters so much, and it changes
into phantasmagoria, only for a man who is on the move; on the
move, for instance, between *cultures*, mobile in more than a physical sense.

When Hardy excels himself, what happens to Hardy the technician? We may recall that the trademark of that technician was an

[8] See, for topography in contemporary American poetry, my lecture, "The
Black Mountain Poets," in Martin Dodsworth (ed.), *The Survival of Poetry*
(London, 1970); also "Geography as Poetic Focus" in *The Southern Review*
IV. 3 (July 1968), pp. 685-91.

often intricate symmetry between stanzas. And if we are right about that, we can begin to answer the question by noticing that both of the admirable poems by Hardy quoted in this chapter are conspicuously asymmetrical. Another finely asymmetrical poem is "The Voice," as we have noticed. And yet there are very few such poems by Hardy. If it is true, as I think it is, that we see him excel himself when he breaks stanzaic symmetry, we cannot expect to have that breaking away into asymmetry manifested for us, as it is in these poems, by the look of the verse on the page. We must learn to look through apparent symmetry to the real asymmetry beneath. Let us look at the body of Hardy's poems which can be designated, in some sense, as love lyrics.

One such is "An Upbraiding," which is like "The Haunter" in that it is put in the mouth of the woman's ghost; it is better than "The Haunter" simply because it is more brief, and shaped much more simply. Of other poems supposedly spoken by the woman, the most imperiously "engineered" is "A Man Was Drawing Near To Me," the most winning is "I Rose and Went To Rou'tor Town," and the most painful is "Love Lost":

> I play my sweet old airs—
> The airs he knew
> When our love was true—
> But he does not balk
> His determined walk,
> And passes up the stairs.
>
> I sing my songs once more,
> And presently hear
> His footstep near
> As if it would stay;
> But he goes his way,
> And shuts a distant door.
>
> So I wait for another morn,
> And another night
> In this soul-sick blight;
> And I wonder much
> As I sit, why such
> A woman as I was born!

There are many poems like this, mostly short, mostly remorseful, written immediately out of the torments that Hardy and Emma inflicted on each other through the last twenty years of their life together. It is distasteful to have to admit that of recent years the biographers, picking apart the cloak of Hardy's reticence, have helped us greatly with small but important poems such as this.[9] These poems are not conspicuously engineered, and taken together they make up a notable achievement. They are of a sort that is nowadays called "confessional," and often esteemed very highly. Indeed, we sometimes hear it said that such poetry, which seems to be written immediately out of the jangle of agonized nerves, is the only poetry that nowadays we can afford to attend to. There are those of us who cannot agree, for whom such confessional poetry is a valid and valuable kind but not the highest. In Hardy's generation Patmore, a headstrong and too fervent critic, nevertheless makes the case for us in his essay, "Emotional Art" (Essay V of *Principle in Art*), when he insists, traditionally enough, on the importance for high art of *repose*—something that confessional poetry by its nature cannot attain to. Thus, to call these poems "painful" is to recognize their achievement but also to limit it. To see that limit transcended, we need only turn to "My Spirit Will Not Haunt the Mound":

> My spirit will not haunt the mound
>   Above my breast,
> But travel, memory-possessed,
> To where my tremulous being found
>   Life largest, best.
>
> My phantom-footed shape will go
>   When nightfall grays
> Hither and thither along the ways

---

[9] A far from exhaustive list would be: "The Rift," "Once at Swanage," "Without, not Within Her," "I Look into My Glass," "You Were the Sort that Men Forget," "Lost Love," "The End of the Episode," "Tolerance," "The Last Performance," "The Peace-Offering," "The Prophetess," "The Walk," "Without Ceremony."

> I and another used to know
> In backward days.
>
> And there you'll find me, if a jot
> You still should care
> For me, and for my curious air;
> If otherwise, then I shall not,
> For you, be there.

Yvor Winters points very justly to "the very quiet and very skillful final stanza." Just so. Between "very skillful" and "brilliantly
engineered" there is a world of difference, and most of the difference is in "quiet." Multiple meanings crowd in upon the word
"curious." And the last lines, by confessing that the ghost is only
subjectively real, forestall objections that must be made to the use
of the ghost convention in inferior poems like "The Haunter."
The completeness of the loss, the irremediable finality of it, is insisted on no less in this poem than in others more painful; the fact
of its being irremediable, which is the source of the pain, is also,
paradoxically, the reason for repose. The poem recognizes this
paradox, as the more painful poems do not; we know that it does
so chiefly by the way that its movement—syntax and meter inter-
woven—works upon us.

Of such poems by Hardy, Irving Howe has said finely:

> These have been called poems of mourning, and so they are. But
> they are also something else, perhaps more valuable. Hardy's ulti-
> mate concern is not with any immediate emotion, but with the
> consequences of emotion, survival beyond emotion: how a man
> lives through what it seems he cannot, and how he learns not to
> tamper with his grief and not even to seek forgiveness in his own
> eyes. The kindness Hardy characteristically shows to all creatures
> he does not deny to himself, for he is free of that version of pride
> which consists in relentless self-accusation. The speaker in these
> poems is a man, perhaps a little better or a little worse than
> others, but not, in any ultimate reckoning, very different. He
> moves through emotion, for there is no way to live and avoid that,
> but then he moves a little past it, toward the salvage of poise. And
> thereby this figure free of the impulse to moralize becomes a
> moral example, such as few among the more brilliant or complex
> sensibilities of our age could provide.

This I take to be a valuable gloss on Coventry Patmore's "repose."

Thus it may appear that we have a rule of thumb by which to recognize Hardy's best love poems: they will be poems in which repose transcends pain (or pleasure, for that matter—but in Hardy that is seldom the problem[10]) as human skill transcends technique.

"After a Journey," for instance, has been singled out for praise by nearly all commentators in the years since F. R. Leavis examined it memorably in *Scrutiny*.[11] And yet there is a general reluctance to locate the convincingness of this poem in the aspect of it where, surely, the conviction is most carried—that is to say, in the meter. For this is, of all Hardy's poems, the one that most triumphantly vindicates the plea he entered for himself in his comment about "the Gothic art-principle in which he had been trained." The "cunning irregularity," achieved by "metrical pauses, and reversed beats," permeates this poem from first to last; it is not to be located in this "touch" or in that, and accordingly —so far is it from being *appliqué* or deftly engineered—we experience it no longer as technical expertise, but as human and as it were manual skill, as "fingering." With that word, we seek our analogies no longer in architecture, but in music; and this is very significant. For Edmund Blunden's deceptively casual chapter on

---

[10] Seldom, and yet sometimes. For instance, "Louie":

> I am forgetting Louie the buoyant;
> Why not raise her phantom, too,
>   Here in daylight
>   With the elect one's?
> She will never thrust the foremost figure out of view!
>
> Mid this heat, in gauzy muslin
> See I Louie's life-lit brow
>   Here in daylight
>   By the elect one's—
> Long two strangers they and far apart; such neighbours now!

Though the scene is a graveyard, here the repose is radiant.

[11] *Scrutiny*, Vol. XIX, No. 2 (1952-3).

Hardy's poems is nowhere so perceptive as when he compares
Hardy's practice in verse with Gautier's "L'Art":

> Oui, l'œuvre sort plus belle
> D'une forme au travail
>   Rebelle,
> Vers, marbre, onyx, émail . . .

For Hardy, as we see from his choosing the architectural analogy,
is, like Gautier, one of the late nineteenth-century poets who find
analogies for their art in the arts that dispose masses in space not
(as music does) in time. And yet, in "After a Journey," the archi-
tectonic symmetries between stanzas, though they persist exactly
and the sensitive prosodist can elicit them,[12] are so overlaid by
cunning irregularities that what we apprehend is the musical form
shaped in time from first through to last, not the architectural
form which reproduces a shape three times over. The rigid symmetry, though it holds firm and could be disclosed by sufficiently
erudite scansion, cedes—in our experience of the poem as we read
it—to the fluid, musical, and narrative shape of the poem as it
starts, goes on, and ends. One remembers, very much to the point,
how Leavis was driven to a musical analogy—"the exquisite modulation into the last stanza"—in the case of a comparable piece,

[12] So I must suppose, at any rate; though I've met no one yet who could scan
the poem. The best I can do is to scan the lines as four-foot trochaic-dactylic.
But the 4th line of the last stanza does not conform. And the short 7th line
has two feet in the first two stanzas, three feet in the later two. Hardy tells
us that he "spent some time in hunting up Latin hymns at the British Mu-
seum," hoping to "enrich" English prosody "by adapting some of the verse-
forms of these." We may note that, according to Schipper (*History of English
Versification*, 1910), tail-rhymed and other elaborate stanza forms may have
come into English from Provençal as well as from Latin hymns. Thus Pound's
Provençal interests would have enabled him to respond readily to the many
elaborate stanzas in Hardy which ask to be analyzed in terms like *frons* and
cauda. I suspect now that the whole of "After a Journey," except for the
penultimate "bob" line in each stanza, is to be understood as written in English hendecasyllables.

"The Voice." And as for the reposefulness of the irremediable, "After a Journey" almost spells it out:

> Trust me, I mind not, though Life lours,
> The bringing me here; nay, bring me here again!

It is a great poem, and it is phantasmagoria:

> Hereto I come to view a voiceless ghost;
> Whither, O whither will its whim now draw me?
> Up the cliff, down, till I'm lonely, lost,
> And the unseen waters' ejaculations awe me.
> Where you will next be there's no knowing,
> Facing round about me everywhere,
> With your nut-coloured hair,
> And gray eyes, and rose-flush coming and going.
>
> Yes: I have re-entered your olden haunts at last;
> Through the years, through the dead scenes I have tracked
> you;
> What have you now found to say of our past—
> Scanned across the dark space wherein I have lacked you?
> Summer gave us sweets, but autumn wrought division?
> Things were not lastly as firstly well
> With us twain, you tell?
> But all's closed now, despite Time's derision.
>
> I see what you are doing: you are leading me on
> To the spots we knew when we haunted here together,
> The waterfall, above which the mist-bow shone
> At the then fair hour in the then fair weather,
> And the cave just under, with a voice still so hollow
> That it seems to call out to me from forty years ago,
> When you were all aglow,
> And not the thin ghost that I now frailly follow!
>
> Ignorant of what there is flitting here to see,
> The waked birds preen and the seals flop lazily;
> Soon you will have, Dear, to vanish from me,
> For the stars close their shutters and the dawn whitens
> hazily.

Trust me, I mind not, though Life lours,
    The bringing me here; nay, bring me here again!
        I am just the same as when
Our days were a joy, and our paths through flowers.

"The Going," written the previous year (1912), is often grouped
with "After a Journey" and "The Voice"—for instance by Douglas
Brown. I am inclined to think of it, rather, as the most ambitious
and memorable of the poems that I have called "confessional" and
"painful." It is very elaborately symmetrical indeed, on a twofold
alternating plan, seven verse lines taking one shape in stanzas 1,
3 and 5, and another in stanzas 2, 4, 6. Given a pattern thus rock-
ing and repetitive, it is very difficult for us to feel the poem unfolding itself, moving us through from first to last, as "After a Journey"
does. And yet Hardy seems to have intended the poem to end, as
it were, quite a long way from where it began. The "Going" of
the title is picked up by "be gone" in the first stanza; this is linked
with "your great going" in the next; and all these variations on
"go" and "going" and "gone" are consummated six lines from the
end in the utterly characteristic, audacious, and harrowing line:
"Unchangeable. It must go." It asks a poet, not just a great and
daring technician, to ring such changes on so common a word, and
by his changes to graph the progress of a pain from first to last
through his poem. And yet if this is the nerve of the poem, the
hidden form of its unfolding, that form is (I think) not merely
hidden and decently cloaked but positively *impeded* by the overt
form with its intricate symmetries. Accordingly, though with the
greatest hesitation, I find the imperious verbal engineer still, even
here, thwarting the true and truly suffering poet.

On the other hand, as nearly every critic has agreed, there can
be no doubt at all about "During Wind and Rain." This is one of
Hardy's greatest achievements. The characteristically exact and
intricate symmetry between the four elaborate stanzas of this
poem is transcended, as it is in the four stanzas of "After a Journey," by the cunning variations of the accomplished metrist; but
the crucial variation can be located and identified, whereas in

"After a Journey" it works all through and all over. In "During Wind and Rain" the variation that is decisive is on the seventh and last line of each stanza:

> "How the sick leaves reel down in throngs!"
>
> "See, the white storm-birds wing across!"
>
> "And the rotten rose is ript from the wall"
>
> "Down their carved names the rain-drop ploughs."

Rhythmically so various, the lines are metrically identical. Though anapaests are twice substituted for iambs in the line about the rose, the expectation of symmetry proves that this line too is iambic tetrameter like the others. And the rhythmical variations testify only to a wonderfully fine ear,[13] not to any special expertise in prosody; in other words, to a human skill, not technical virtuosity. The effect is that when we reach the refrain at the end of the third stanza, though symmetry is maintained between that stanza and the first two, it is so masked by the rhythmical variation that, instead of checking back to register how this stanza reproduces the earlier ones, we are propelled forward to see what will happen in the last. And thus we experience an unfolding from first to last, not a folding back three times over. The feeling flows into each stanza, brims, and three times pours into the next. Repose transcends pain, as manual skill transcends mechanical technique.

There are other poems by Hardy of which one wants to speak admiringly in such terms. One is "Beeny Cliff," and another is "At Castle Boterel," in which the musical flow through the symmetrically sculpted stanzas is signalized with unusual plainness, by a carry-over of sense and grammar from the first stanza to the second. But it is more important to insist that these poems to which we give unqualified praise are, when all is said and done, thoroughly of a piece with others about which we have qualms or

---

[13] I am sorry and surprised to find Irving Howe perpetuating an old error when he says of Hardy: "His ear was uncertain: many of his lines drag and crumble . . ." (Howe, *Thomas Hardy*, pp. 162-63).

hesitations. On the one hand this means (to reiterate) that we cannot add to the list of thoroughly approved pieces until we arrive at a Selected Poems that will stand in place of the Collected. For the range—or, better still, the *ranging-ness*—of Hardy's imaginative activity is one of the most impressive things about him, and no weeding out of imperfections can be allowed to obscure this. On the other hand, when we find Hardy excelling himself, this is not quite the same as saying that he transcends himself and those professed principles of his which we have called "liberal" and "scientific humanist." It still matters that the gods in Hardy's phantasmagoria are all ghosts. The apparition of the dead Emma in "After a Journey" is certainly not conventional, like the apparition of Wolsey in "A Spellbound Palace"; but this doesn't mean that the experience recorded in the poem should have been submitted to the Society for Psychical Research. And indeed, if the Hardy of 1922, the scientific humanist, were to say that the apparition and the dialogue in "After a Journey" were only a manner of speaking, we should not need to quarrel with him.

This must be my excuse for trying to connect Hardy with his younger contemporaries, Pasternak and Pound. Though we can find things that they have in common with him, in the end what must strike us is how different he is. Pound and Pasternak (and Yeats and G. M. Hopkins and Eliot) are radical in a sense that Hardy isn't. All these other poets claim, by implication or else explicitly, to give us entry through their poems into a world that is truer and more real than the world we know from statistics or scientific induction or common sense. Their criticism of life is radical in that they refuse to accept life on the terms in which it offers itself, and has to be coped with, through most of the hours of every day. In their poems, that quotidian reality is transformed, displaced, supplanted; the alternative reality which their poems create is offered to us as a superior reality, by which the reality of every day is to be judged and governed. But neither in "After a Journey" nor anywhere else does Hardy make that claim. For him, "criticism of life" means "application of ideas to life"—the two formulations by Matthew Arnold are two ways of saying the same thing. And so his poems, instead of transforming and displacing quantifiable reality or the reality of common sense, are on the contrary just so many glosses on that reality, which is conceived of as unchallengeably "given" and final. This is what makes it possible to say (once again) that he sold the vocation short, tacitly surrendering the proudest claims traditionally made for the act of the poetic imagination. Whether this was inevitable, given his intellectual convictions and the state of the world in his time, is an interesting question. Some poems by a later atheist and scientific humanist, Hugh MacDiarmid, suggest that it was not. In any case, it happened; and the consequences of it, for some of Hardy's successors, have been momentous.

～3～

Landscapes of Larkin

Let there be treaties, bridges,
    Chords under the hands, to be spanned
Sustained: extremity hates a given good
    Or a good gained. That girl who took
Her life almost, then wrote a book
    To exorcise and to exhibit the sin,
Praises a friend there for the end she made
    And each of them becomes a heroine.
The time is in love with endings. The time's
    Spoiled children threaten what they will do,
And those they cannot shake by petulance
    They'll bribe out of their wits by show.[1]

I shall take it for granted that Philip Larkin is a very Hardyesque poet; that Hardy has been indeed the determining influence in Larkin's career, once he had overcome a youthful infatuation with Yeats. Larkin has testified to that effect repeatedly, and any open-minded reader of the poems of the two men must recognize many resemblances, though Larkin, it is true, has shown himself a poet of altogether narrower range—it is only a part of Hardy that is perpetuated by Larkin into the 1960s, but it is a central and important part.

The narrowness of range, and the slenderness of Larkin's record

[1] Charles Tomlinson, "Against Extremity," *The Way of a World* (London, 1969). The allusion appears to be to Anne Sexton and the late Sylvia Plath.

63

so far (three slim collections of poems, and of those only two that are relevant) might seem to suggest that he cannot bear the weight of significance that I want to put on him, as the central figure in English poetry over the last twenty years. But in fact there has been the widest possible agreement, over most of this period, that Philip Larkin is for good or ill the effective unofficial laureate of post-1945 England. Some may have criticized what Larkin does with the truths he discovers, what attitudes he takes up to the landscapes and the weather of his own poems; but those landscapes and that weather—no one, I think, has failed to recognize them. And this is just as true if we think of landscapes and weather metaphorically; we recognize in Larkin's poems the seasons of present-day England, but we recognize also the seasons of an English soul—the moods he expresses are our moods too, though we may deal with them differently. On the literal level at any rate, no one denies that what Larkin says is true; that the England in his poems is the England we have inhabited. We may compare Ted Hughes, who—in America especially—is Larkin's chief rival for the unofficial laurels. We all know that England still has bullfrogs and otters and tramps asleep in ditches; yet because in the landscape of Hughes's poems these shaggy features bulk so large, it may strike us as more an Irish landscape than an English one. The congested England that we have inhabited day by day is Larkin's England:

> A slow and stopping curve southwards we kept,
> Wide farms went by, short-shadowed cattle, and
> Canals with floatings of industrial froth;
> A hothouse flashed, uniquely; hedges dipped
> And rose; and now and then a smell of grass
> Displaced the reek of buttoned carriage-cloth
> Until the next town, new and nondescript,
> Approached with acres of dismantled cars.[2]

Those slow canals have wound through many a poem about England since T. S. Eliot's *Waste Land*, but never under such a level

2 Philip Larkin, *The Whitsun Weddings* (New York, 1964).

light as this. For in the poem as a whole ("The Whitsun Weddings"), the tone of the describing voice is scrupulously neutral; it affords no handle at all for reflections like "A canal, not a river," or "Tainted water, not fresh." There is no meaning, no "placing," in the way preindustrial things like farms, cattle, hedges, and grass are interspersed with industrial things like chemical froth and dismantled cars. And for Larkin indeed this seems to be one of the rules of the game; there is to be no historical perspective, no measuring of present against past. Canals and smashed cars come along with hedges and cattle simply because they come along like that in any railway journey through England, as we all know. And precisely because poem after poem since *The Waste Land* has measured our present (usually seen as depleted) against our past (usually seen as rich), Larkin's refusal to do this is thoroughly refreshing—at last, we recognize with relief, we can take all that for granted, take it as read. It's in this that Larkin differs from John Betjeman, whom he admires; Betjeman is the most nostalgic of poets, Larkin the least.

And yet this poet who speaks so levelly of "Canals with floatings of industrial froth" is the author also of "Water":

> If I were called in
> To construct a religion
> I should make use of water.
>
> Going to church
> Would entail a fording
> To dry, different clothes;
>
> The litany would employ
> Images of sousing
> A furious devout drench.
>
> And I would raise in the east
> A glass of water
> Where any-angled light
> Would congregate endlessly.[3]

[3] Philip Larkin, *The Whitsun Weddings.*

This is less distinctive writing than "The Whitsun Weddings," but not therefore less distinguished. And the mere fact of its existence proves, if proof be needed, that when Larkin in more ambitious pieces refuses to recognize any special dignity or sanctity attached to elemental presences like water, it is not because this sort of sentiment about the natural is foreign to his experience. He mostly refuses to allow such sentiments into the peopled landscapes of his England because they would impede his level-toned acceptance of that England as the only one we have, violated and subtopianized and poisoned as it is. To put it more pointedly, Larkin makes himself numb to the nonhuman creation in order to stay compassionate towards the human. Thus, near the end of "The Whitsun Weddings," when

> I thought of London spread out in the sun,
> Its postal districts packed like squares of wheat . . .

the collision between the organicism of wheat and the rigidity of "postal districts" is calculated. It is the human pathos of the many weddings he has seen from the train which spills over to sanctify, for the poet, the postal districts of London, the train's destination; the human value suffuses the abstractly schematized with the grace of an organic fertility.

This makes Larkin into one sort of extreme humanist. And no doubt it lays him open to the antihumanist objection which, for instance, Leo Shestov brought against Chekhov, that if so little is asked of the human person before he deserves sympathy, then the sympathy is not worth having. If the persons in the landscape were thought to be in some degree the makers as well as the victims of the history which has polluted the landscape round them, they would gain in dignity by just as much as they forfeited compassion. What cannot be doubted, I think, is that Larkin has foreseen this objection and decided to risk it; that he does not lower his sights without counting beforehand those experiences (for instance, natural piety about water) which, when the sights are lowered, must go out of focus.

Larkin therefore would understand, though he might not like, a poem called "Hardly Anything Bears Watching" by Mairi Mac-Innes:

> Hardly anything bears watching.
> Bricks and stone
> Have lost their intense surprise.
> For years I kept my trust in things.
>
> Even beyond the last parishes
> Fringed with refuse,
> Hills drawn beneath the surveyor's rod.
> They too lie perfectly numb.
>
> The old parabolas of socialism,
> Spirals of love,
> Make hope the habitat of the soul.
> But hope's not native to the blood.
>
> No comfort from the boy who draws
> Upon my memory of bombs.
> The man recalls
> Brave days on a far-off sea.
>
> Picture after picture fails.
> When I was young,
> The pavement kerbs were made of stone,
> A substance like my finger-nails.
>
> It is not like that any more.
> I do not see
> The essential life of inorganic things.
> Humanity has covered all.[4]

In this surely admirable poem, it is once again the curiously level tone of voice which can carry off the big blunt words like "inorganic" and "humanity" and "hope" and "the soul." Mairi Mac-Innes is counting the cost more explicitly than Larkin does; and rather plainly in the lines about "The old parabolas of socialism" she comes nearer repenting of her bargain than ever Larkin does—

[4] Mairi MacInnes, "Hardly Anything Bears Watching," quoted from *The Spectator*, August 16, 1963.

though for that matter I have my own ideas about what causes the powerfully ugly and vicious poems that our laureate sometimes disconcerts us with, poems like "A Study of Reading Habits" or "Send No Money." Miss MacInnes's poem says that to buy sympathy with the human, at the price of alienation from the nonhuman, is a hard bargain at best.

However, not many English poets think so. For most of them, "nature poetry" (since that after all is what we are talking about) is a world well lost. The reviewer who said that Ted Hughes's "Pike" was at bottom a Georgian nature poem thought he had scored a shrewd hit. And conversely, when A. Alvarez (introducing the Penguin *New Poetry*) wants to establish that Hughes's poem about horses is better than Larkin's "At Grass," on the same subject, he does so to his own satisfaction by arguing that Hughes's poem isn't about horses at all; that the horses are "symbolic"—and symbolic of what? Why, of something in the human psyche, of course. In other words, it's only when what seems to be a nature poem can be converted into a human-nature poem that we begin to take it seriously. This is a humanism like Larkin's, but less respectable because it does not count the cost, seems not to know that there is any cost incurred. A poem by Alvarez proceeds on the same assumption—an account of the killing of an animal by a drinking pool is deliberately blurred into an evocation of the sexual act between two people; in other words, the encounter between human and nonhuman has no value and no significance until it can be made an allegory of an encounter between humans. One recalls the cries of satisfaction with which the modern reader approaches that one of Wordsworth's nature poems, "Nutting," in which the imagery conveys a submerged metaphor of rape. "All value is in the human, and nowhere else." It is a possible point of view, and may be sincerely held. For the English it has the great advantage of anesthetizing them to the offensiveness of their own landscapes and removing any sense of guilt at having made them offensive. It is D. H. Lawrence's constant guilt and horror at what the English had made of England which makes it certain that, breeder as he was of his own symbolic horses (in *The Rainbow*, in

St. Mawr), he certainly counted the cost and mostly he thought it extortionate.

Kingsley Amis, an Englishman in Wales, sets the scene for the amours of Mr. Evans and Mrs. Rhys in "Aberdarcy, the Main Square":

> The journal of some bunch of architects
> Named this the worst town centre they could find;
> But how disparage what so well reflects
> Permanent tendencies of heart and mind?
>
> All love demands a witness: something "there"
> Which it yet makes part of itself. These two
> Might find Carlton House Terrace, St. Mark's Square,
> A bit on the grand side. What about you?[5]

This is not a level tone at all. The ugliness that it is, piled on to the ugliness it talks about, sets us veering crazily between disgust and self-disgust as we oscillate without guidance between the two possible answers to the last question. Either, "Yes, I too should find it too grand (or too beautiful)"—in which case we confess that our own amours, and by implication everybody's, are as squalid and furtive as Evans's; or else, "No, I deserve something better than Aberdarcy"—in which case we are being superior and unfeeling toward the Evanses of the world, and perhaps hypocritical as well.

It is the same dilemma—either we accept that we deserve no better than the gracelessness of scene which surrounds us, or else we shut ourselves off from our neighbors who seem to ask nothing better and are doing their best to make it worse. Like Richard Hoggart as regards literature, Larkin, as regards landscape and architecture and indeed literature also, agrees to tolerate the intolerable for the sake of human solidarity with those who don't find it intolerable at all. Rather than put up with the intolerable, Lawrence forfeited the solidarity—and with a clearer sense of what he was doing, of the price he was paying. As for Amis, he leaves us to

[5] Kingsley Amis, "Aberdarcy, the Main Square," *A Look Round the Estate* (New York, 1968).

answer a question he cannot answer himself. Exploiting the facile
irony of that veering tone which Auden reinvented for us, he contrives to be, in the brilliantly baleful words of Auden himself,
"paid on both sides"—though in a devalued currency. And this is
the irony so readily applauded in British writing today; it refuses
to answer questions which need answering.

To give Amis his due, the question he asks is no longer open by
the time he has finished with it; at the end of his sequence, "The
Evans Country," he contrives (though in wretchedly bad writing)
an effect of hysterical brutality which leaves us still in the dark
about Evans's motives, but not about Amis's attitude to him. The
last two stanzas of "Welch Ferry, West Side" can only mean that
we are all alike, each of us is Evans at heart, and none of us therefore deserves anything better than Aberdarcy:

> . . . all the smog had lifted, and more stars
> Than he knew what to do with filled the sky,
> And lighted lighthouse, civic centre, quay,
> Chimneys, the pony's pasture, cooling-towers;
> "Looks beautiful tonight," he muttered,
>
> Then raised his voice: "Eurwen, get moving, do,
> You think I want to hang round here all night?
> Free over the week-end, are you? I'm not;
> I'm boozing with the boys on Saturday,
> Sunday's the club . . . All right, then—never."[6]

The self-disgust of this crowds out compassion; yet in his twisted
way Amis too opts for solidarity—St. Mark's, with all the grace
and grandeur of an architectural setting fit for human action of
dignity, is the price that must be paid for fellow feeling with the
Evanses.

And all this has political implications. There is nothing gratui-
tous about Mairi MacInnes's word, "socialism." For this readiness
to opt in the last resort for solidarity at all costs, to trade the nonhuman for the human, to lose dignity and beauty and elegance for

---

[6] Kingsley Amis, A Look Round the Estate.

the sake of supposedly more tangible and general benefits—this is the distinguishing mark of the British Left. Indeed, in the astonishing way that life has of imitating literature, Amis's sequence on his squalid amorist Evans was no sooner published than we saw English intellectuals of the Left making the late Stephen Ward (one of the minor actors in the Profumo scandal) into love's martyr, happy to overlook the squalid tastelessness of his life as a procurer for the sake of the humaneness which (arguably) shone through it. And if this is the choice of the Left, the only possible alternative—a moral fastidiousness which cannot help but seem arrogant—certainly finds no home in the British Conservative party; it must look for its politics much further to the Right, as the case of Lawrence shows. In fact, I suppose, all parliamentary politics in Britain belongs in the broad band of the political Center, which corresponds to the ironist's evasion of the choice, his wish to be paid on both sides though at reduced rates—and just as well perhaps, for the open-minded ironist is worth more in politics than he is in poetry. (And that's a reflection to make any poet pause and disconsolately wonder.)

Looked at in this way, Larkin's poetry of lowered sights and patiently diminished expectations can be justified, and the British poetic scene in which he figures makes no bad showing. Larkin and others like him, in the '50s and '60s, seem to have been facing, in different ways and with different degrees of honesty and awareness, an issue which the anthologists and editors and commentators of that period hardly perceived at all. And of course this is as it should be—the respectable poets should always be several jumps ahead of their readers. (And yet throughout the period there was a common and totally unacceptable assumption that there existed an English audience—a mass audience, said the Left; an *élite*, said the Right—which deserved better poets than it was getting.)

Commentary came nearest engaging with this issue that concerned the poets when, in the early 1960s, it began to consider the allegation that writing like Larkin's was damagingly insular and provincial. At different levels of urbanity and perceptiveness this was discussed in Robert Conquest's introduction to his anthology,

New Lines 2 (London, 1963), in Alvarez's introduction to his anthology, *The New Poetry* (Harmondsworth, 1962; 2nd ed., 1966), and in John Press's *Rule and Energy* (London, 1963). But none of these approached the question at the level that seems to be called for; nor did the medicine prescribed and rather timidly taken—respectful reading of foreign poets in translation, and of some Americans—seem to cure the disease, if disease was what it was. For surely the distinctive quality and the distinctive task of poetry in Britain were defined, and are still to be defined, by the fact that Britain as a whole is the most industrialized landscape in the world; that there the nonhuman has been exploited and violated by the human more consistently and over a longer period than anywhere else. It was English poetry (with Wordsworth) that in modern times first expressed ideas of elemental sanctity and natural piety; and it seems it must be English poetry which asks what to do with these ideas in a landscape where virtually all the sanctuaries have been violated, all the pieties blasphemed. Though this is essentially a British theme, it is not therefore insular. For industrialization, with the suburbia that is its corollary, is coming to other parts of the globe only a little less fast than it has come to England and South Wales, Northern Ireland and much of Scotland. Larkin, who deals with this issue (explicitly in "Water," obliquely in "The Whitsun Weddings"), may be insular in other ways; but certainly this theme of his is central to the contemporary experience of readers far outside the British Isles.

The difficulty of confronting this theme in poetry cannot be overestimated. The poet confronts it even when he writes on quite other themes, for he knows it in the damage it has done to the language he has to use. Our poetry suffers from the loss, or the drastic impoverishment, of the traditional images of celebration. Consider only Larkin's images of this kind, wheat and water; or Mairi Mac-Innes's image, worked stone ("The pavement kerbs were made of stone"). Can we believe that it makes no difference to the potency of these ancient images, when more and more, as poets and readers, we know water only as it flows from a tap; when we can go from one year's end to the next without seeing a wheatfield, and when the bread we eat—chemically blanched, ready-sliced, untouched by human hand—bears no perceivable relation to the wheat-ear; when we walk and live no longer amid stone but amid concrete? Can we trust any longer the celebratory, hallowing potency which these images and others like them (laurel and nightingale, rose and oak) have manifested in poetry of the past? It is questions like these that are involved when one conceives of a poetry that should survive in a wholly urbanized and industrialized society. And if, as seems likely, it is British poets who are called on first to write such a poetry, their task is dauntingly difficult. A poem such as "The Whitsun Weddings," though it may be written from a standpoint we cannot endorse, is heartening evidence of how the British poet might rise to this historically unprecedented challenge.

The foregoing pages on Larkin, except for some touchings up and second thoughts, were already in print in 1963, when I had not begun to think about the significance of Hardy for the English poets who came after him. But plainly what I have called Larkin's lowering of his sights represents a further withdrawal or surrender beyond those that Hardy had made already. And yet Larkin has more excuse than Hardy, so much excuse that we cannot in justice call him a cop-out, though plenty of people have done so. If his range is obviously narrower than Hardy's, in the sector that we are concerned with his analysis goes, or is pushed by historical circumstances, much deeper. As concerned as Hardy is with landscape, he never, so far as I know, confronts the exploitation and poisoning of landscape by industry. On the one hand he could not do so because of his ambiguous sympathy with technology and with his sense of himself as technician. (And, incidentally, there is nothing of this in Larkin—the stanzaic and metrical symmetries which he mostly aims at are achieved skillfully enough, but with none of that bristling expertise of Hardy which sets itself, and surmounts, intricate technical challenges.) On the other hand, the landscapes of Hardy's England were not yet quailing so defenselessly before technology as they are now, after fifty years of the cheap motor car. And this rape of the sanctuaries provokes in Larkin a sense for what has been ravished—the elemental sanctity of water and wheat, something else that Hardy never invokes, devout Wordsworthian though he was. (Would he have thought it one sort of belief in "the witches of Endor"? One hopes not.)

But it is in the political implications of their poetry that the two poets are most alike. Each of them settles for parliamentary democracy as a shabby, unavoidable second-best. Do they persuade us that it is indeed unavoidable? Larkin apparently does not persuade Colin Falck.[7] Mr. Falck, taking issue with my essay of 1963 (though really it is Larkin he is quarreling with), declares at the end of a careful scrutiny of Larkin's poems:

> In rejecting Larkin's particular brand of "humanism" I may seem to be asking for the kind of "right wing" violence to which D. H. Lawrence was sometimes led. I think perhaps I am. The last and truest humanism in art is the truthful expression of emotion, and this is something prior to all questions of politics: it concerns only the honesty or the corruption of our consciousness. If this means barbarism, then let us have barbarism.

Falck goes on to say that barbarism "has come to be associated with obscurity," whereas what he asks for is "lucid barbarism"—which forces me to recognize that I don't know what "barbarism" means as he uses the word. More mysteriously still, he says of this lucid barbarism, "If we cannot face it in art, we shall have to face it soon enough in life," then speaks in his next sentence of "this post-Nazi age." My mystification is complete; for I should have thought that the experience we have had, thanks to the Nazis, of what a right-wing alternative to parliamentary democracy is like—an experience available to Larkin but not to Hardy—is what should impel us to acknowledge that the shabby second-best we have is indeed unavoidably our choice, the alternative having turned out so much worse. The alternatives currently on offer of course come not from the Right but the Left; and one would like to know what

[7] Colin Falck, "Philip Larkin," *The Review*, No. 14, reprinted in *The Modern Poet: Essays from The Review*, ed. by Ian Hamilton (London, 1968), pp. 101-10.

Colin Falck thinks of *their* violence. But in fact I think he is speaking of a violence that has nothing to do with political arrangements at all: a barbarism and a violence merely of rhetoric and gesture. One does not have to be any sort of dogmatic Marxist to be dumbfounded when he asserts that "the last and truest humanism in art" is "prior to all questions of politics." How can this be so? That "truthful expression of emotion" which he asks for has to express the emotion of an individual, the poet. And is not that individual conditioned, at least in part, by the politics he lives among and has suffered through? Are the emotions which Larkin seeks to express in no way conditioned by his being a post-Nazi poet, whereas Thomas Hardy wasn't? Hardy and Larkin, it appears, accept responsibility for the political implications of what they say in their poems; and Colin Falck wishes they wouldn't. Indeed the poet, as Falck conceives of him, is a highly specialized creature. For he has said earlier in his essay:

> No doubt it is always important to maintain some general sense
> of what most other people's lives are like. But the poet cannot
> be content with this, and it might even be argued that it is not
> really his business *qua* poet at all, whatever might be expected
> of him as a novelist or as a human being.

Hardy and Larkin may have sold poetry short; but at least neither of them sold it so short as to make the poet less than a human being. And part of being human is being a citizen of some commonwealth. I can sympathize with Falck's outraged refusal of the diminished world which Larkin's poetry proffers as the only one available to him; but he cannot escape that world as easily as he thinks.

I don't know that any of us can escape it. I have spent some time on Colin Falck only to introduce a far more sustained and tormented attempt to break out of the grayly constricting world of Larkin, and (I fear we must say) the not much less constricting world of Hardy. This attempt has been Charles Tomlinson's. Ever since 1957 Tomlinson has been lucidly angry at what he pungently calls the "suburban mental ratio" which Larkin and other poets

have imposed on their experience. And he has not failed to realize
that his quarrel with these contemporaries is in part a political
quarrel, or at least that it has immediate political implications. He
has written, for instance, with evident and explicit sympathy,
about the *élitist* and hierarchical politics which W. B. Yeats was
drawn to from his youth when he responded with enthusiasm to
Nietzsche.[8] It is the more remarkable that, as I read him, Tomlinson has lately—though with unabated anger and contempt—settled
for Larkin's world as indeed *politically* the only one that we dare
conceive of for ourselves. This is the acknowledgment he makes at
the end of "Prometheus":

> Summer thunder darkens, and its climbing
>   Cumulae, disowning our scale in the zenith,
> Electrify this music: the evening is falling apart.
>   Castles-in-air; on earth: green, livid fire.
> The radio simmers with static to the strains
>   Of this mock last-day of nature and of art.
>
> We have lived through apocalypse too long:
>   Scriabin's dinosaurs! Trombones for the transformation
> That arrived by train at the Finland Station,
>   To bury its hatchet after thirty years in the brain
> Of Trotsky. Alexander Nikolayevitch, the events
>   Were less merciful than your mob of instruments.
>
> Too many drowning voices cram this waveband.
>   I set Lenin's face by yours—
> Yours, the fanatic ego of eccentricity against
>   The systematic son of a schools inspector
> Tyutchev on desk—for the strong man reads
>   Poets as the antisemite pleads: "A Jew was my friend."
>
> Cymballed firesweeps. Prometheus came down
>   In more than orchestral flame and Kérensky fled

[8] See Tomlinson, "Yeats and the Practising Poet," in *An Honoured Guest*,
ed. by Denis Donoghue and J. R. Mulryne (London, 1965), pp. 1-7. Predictably, Hardy felt for Nietzsche nothing but contempt; see Hardy's letters to
the press in 1914, reprinted in *Life and Art*, ed. by Ernest Brennecke (New
York, 1925), pp. 137-39.

Before it. The babel of continents gnaws now
    And tears at the silk of those harmonies that seemed
So dangerous once. You dreamed an end
    Where the rose of the world would go out like a close in
        music.

Population drags the partitions down
    And we are a single town of warring suburbs:
I cannot hear such music for its consequence:
    Each sense was to have been reborn
Out of a storm of perfumes and light
    To a white world, an in-the-beginning.

In the beginning, the strong man reigns:
    Trotsky, was it not then you brought yourself
To judgement and to execution, when you forgot
    Where terror rules, justice turns arbitrary?
Chromatic Prometheus, myth of fire,
    It is history topples you in the zenith.

Blok, too, wrote The Scythians
    Who should have known: he who howls
With the whirlwind, with the whirlwind goes down.
    In this, was Lenin guiltier than you
When, out of a merciless patience grew
    The daily prose such poetry prepares for?

Scriabin, Blok, men of extremes,
    History treads out the music of your dreams
Through blood, and cannot close like this
    In the perfection of anabasis. It stops. The trees
Continue raining though the rain has ceased
    In a cooled world of incessant codas:

Hard edges of the houses press
    On the after-music senses, and refuse to burn,
Where an ice-cream van circulates the estate
    Playing Greensleeves, and at the city's
Stale new frontier even ugliness
    Rules with the cruel mercy of solidities.[9]

This is not Tomlinson's characteristic style. The poem is in a collection called *The Way of a World* (1969), and the only British

[9] Charles Tomlinson, "Prometheus," *The Way of a World.*

reviewer who did justice to the book rightly remarked, in "Prometheus" and some other poems, "a less private voice, a controlled rhetoric which claims and commands a wider space, ranges over a more impressive variety of tones than ever before."[10] But though his more characteristic style is different from this, it is no nearer than this to any style that could be called Hardyesque. Tomlinson's styles always transform and displace the realities known to science, to statistics, to the bleared eye of every day; he refuses the Hardyesque surrender, by which those realities are the unquestionable texts which poetry can only gloss. Tomlinson is a poet for whom an expression like "one thought cuts through another with clean edge" is abundantly meaningful. The realm of experience which such an expression refers to, the realm of the *phantastikon*,[11] a realm which Hardy and Larkin infrequently break into without meaning to and without noticing, is the world which Tomlinson's imagination lives in and ranges over continually.

And yet Tomlinson stops short of myth. If he characteristically transforms and displaces quotidian reality, it is not in order to supplant that reality, but on the contrary only to do it justice by defining and following through with patience the articulations of it— articulations which our bleared eyes miss, resonances which our dulled ears slide over without noticing. And it is this tough-minded grasp upon the actual which enables and indeed compels him, here, to settle for the canned music of "Greensleeves" from an ice-cream van, as symbolizing *politically* something at least solid and merciful, whereas Scriabin's tone poem, "Prometheus," orchestrates a politics which has proved itself both merciless (the

---

[10] Ronald Hayman, "Observation Plus," in *Encounter* (December, 1970), p. 73.

[11] See Pound, "Psychology and Troubadours" (1916), now printed as chapter V of Pound's *The Spirit of Romance* (New York reprint, 1968, p. 92): "We have about us the universe of fluid force, and below us the germinal universe of wood alive, of stone alive. Man is—the sensitive physical part of him—a mechanism . . . As to his consciousness, the consciousness of some seems to rest, or to have its center more properly, in what the Greek psychologists called the *phantastikon*. Their minds are, that is, circumvolved about them like soap-bubbles reflecting sundry patches of the macrocosmos."

murder of Trotsky) and nebulous. Thus Tomlinson, when he thinks politically, lowers his sights and settles for second-best just as Larkin and Hardy do—but more impressively than either because so much more aware of, and pained by, the cost.

Hardy, it is true, predicted what the cost would be and was pained by it in prospect: "Democratic government may be justice to man, but it will probably merge in proletarian, and when these people are our masters it will lead to more of this contempt, and possibly be the utter ruin of art and literature!" This marks off Hardy from Larkin very sharply: Hardy moved at ease and as of right in the *bourgeois* culture which he had made his own by strenuous self-education. Catullus and Voltaire, Gibbon and Aeschylus, Clement and Origen, *La Bohème* and *Il Trovatore*, the painters Eddy and Maclise, are named on the pages of Hardy with as little embarrassment as Scriabin and Blok, Van Gogh and Constable and Maillol, are named by Tomlinson. Larkin at best ignores such names, at worst he turns upon them snarling:

> (He once met Morgan Forster) . . .
>
> Books are a load of crap.

In fact on this issue Hardy's gloomy forebodings have not been borne out: it is not the proletarians, "our masters," who have heaped contempt on Hardy's art and literature, but the masters of those masters, the black-leg intellectuals who direct and use "the media" (including, of course, newsprint). It is these, the self-appointed spokesmen for a proletarian culture not theirs, who will not forgive poems like Tomlinson's which are webbed together by specific allusions to music, literature, and history. And their strategy is always the same, apocalyptic; somewhere—on the Somme, in Petrograd, at Katyn or Buchenwald, over Dresden, in Algeria, or at My Lai (the list is endless)—something has happened of such momentous enormity that, so they would persuade us, it has removed our right any longer to frequent the artistic and intellectual monuments of the past, having made those monuments irrelevant to our condition. It is to challenge these apocalyptic voices that

Tomlinson, elsewhere in *The Way of a World*, writes "Against Extremity," declaring "extremity hates a given good/Or a good gained," and "The time is in love with endings." Hardy, especially if we measure him against his contemporary Yeats, is of Tomlinson's way of thinking. But Larkin is a different case. His is not an apocalyptic voice; on the contrary those who fly to extremes cannot forgive him his mostly level tone. And yet, he is certainly in love with endings. Moreover he is so ready to lower his sights—to a point where artistic monuments go out of focus, no less than elemental presences and sanctities—that we begin to think he does so under pressure not from "the age," but only from some compulsion in himself. Certainly, if the lowered sights can be vindicated in "The Whitsun Weddings," there are other poems in which they cannot.

One such poem is "Here," which seems to be a portrait of the city of Hull and its environs:

> Swerving east, from rich industrial shadows
> And traffic all night north; swerving through fields
> Too thin and thistled to be called meadows,
> And now and then a harsh-named halt, that shields
> Workmen at dawn; swerving to solitude
> Of skies and scarecrows, haystacks, hares and pheasants,
> And the widening river's slow presence,
> The piled gold clouds, the shining gull-marked mud,
>
> Gathers to the surprise of a large town:
> Here domes and statues, spires and cranes cluster
> Beside grain-scattered streets, barge-crowded water,
> And residents from raw estates, brought down
> The dead straight miles by stealing flat-faced trolleys,
> Push through plate-glass swing doors to their desires—
> Cheap suits, red kitchen-ware, sharp shoes, iced lollies,
> Electric mixers, toasters, washers, driers—
>
> A cut-price crowd, urban yet simple, dwelling
> Where only salesmen and relations come
> Within a terminate and fishy-smelling
> Pastoral of ships up streets, the slave museum,
> Tattoo-shops, consulates, grim head-scarfed wives;

And out beyond its mortgaged half-built edges
Fast-shadowed wheat-fields, running high as hedges,
Isolate villages, where removed lives

Loneliness clarifies. Here silence stands
Like wheat. Here leaves unnoticed thicken,
Hidden weeds flower, neglected waters quicken,
Luminously-peopled air ascends;
And past the poppies bluish neutral distance
Ends the land suddenly beyond a beach
Of shapes and shingle. Here is unfenced existence:
Facing the sun, untalkative, out of reach.[12]

Here every nonurban thing comes along with a negating or cancel-
ing epithet—leaves are "unnoticed," waters are "neglected," distance is "neutral." And if existence is "unfenced," it is also "out
of reach"; if it is "untalkative," it is by that token noncommittal,
unhelpful. The insistence seems excessive—as if the poet were *determined* not to be helped nor instructed by things that plainly he
responds to keenly. (For obviously the leaves do not go unnoticed
by him, so by whom are they "unnoticed"? By the cut-price crowd,
or by the country dwellers? And if by both or either, is this a good
thing or a bad?) It was not thus that Hardy responded to the
waked birds that preen, the seals that flop lazily, in "After a Journey." And in "Beeny Cliff," though "The woman now is—elsewhere—whom the ambling pony bore,/And nor knows nor cares
for Beeny, and will laugh there never more," it is as a source of
mysterious comfort, not in mocking irrelevance, that "Still in all
its chasmal beauty bulks old Beeny to the sky."

In Larkin's poem one detects a perverse determination that the
ultimate ("terminate") pastoral shall be among the cut-price
stores, and nowhere else. And the pity felt for the denizens of that
pastoral, the "residents from raw estates," is more than a little contemptuous. A political analogue might be the petty bourgeois who,
aspiring to the cultural goods and sylvan retreats of the *haut bourgeois*, finds himself overtaken by the proletarians, and resentfully

---

[12] Philip Larkin, "Here," *The Whitsun Weddings*.

throws in his lot with them, a dedicated iconoclast such as they have no wish to be. This is unfair—it defines some of Larkin's critics more than it defines Larkin; but it shows how little resistance his world, and his cast of mind, can muster against such iconoclasts. If he is Hardy's heir, he sells out or sells off a great deal of his inherited estate. Yet Hardy had provided the precedent for such a sell-out. And of course in the interim between Hardy and Larkin (or Tomlinson) the pressures to make such surrenders had increased.

~ 4 ~

Lucky Jim
and the Hobbits

Forgive me Sire, for cheating your intent,
That I, who should command a regiment,
Do amble amiably here, O God,
One of the neat ones in your awkward squad.[1]

I t would be unfair to Kingsley Amis to leave an account of his
poetry with my rude remarks in the last chapter about "The
Evans Country." In the years before that poem Amis had written
several pieces very cleanly and solidly composed, which are too
little known and too little respected. Amis the novelist, Amis the
polemicist, and latterly Amis the personality on radio and tele-
vision, have crowded out of attention Amis the poet; and this
sufficiently illustrates the relative importance given in modern
Britain to writing in verse, writing in prose, and unconsidered remarks by way of "the media." Amis's poetry, however, is much to
our purpose, since far more than his novels it concerns itself quite
explicitly with political issues. It does so not under Hardyesque
but rather under Gravesian auspices; and so this chapter must be
regarded as a digression—though a necessary one—for the understanding of the climate of political ideas in which British poets
since Hardy have been working.

[1] Norman Cameron, 1905-1953. "Forgive Me, Sire," from his *Collected
Poems* (London, 1957).

83

The political idea that Amis has been particularly concerned with is that crucial one, the concept of authority. For instance:

THE VOICE OF AUTHORITY: A LANGUAGE GAME

Do this. Don't move. O'Grady says do this,
You get a move on, see, do what I say.
Look lively when I say O'Grady says.

Say this. Shut up. O'Grady says say this,
You talk fast without thinking what to say.
What goes is what I say O'Grady says.

Or rather let me put the point like this:
O'Grady says what goes is what I say
O'Grady says; that's what O'Grady says.

By substituting you can shorten this,
Since any god you like will do to say
The things you like, that's what O'Grady says.

The harm lies not in that, but in that this
Progression's first and last terms are I say
O'Grady says, not just O'Grady says.

Yet it's O'Grady must be out of this
Before what we say goes, not what we say
O'Grady says. Or so O'Grady says.[2]

This piece is what it says it is, "A language game." There is an obvious sense in which it isn't a poem. The game "O'Grady," familiar to me from my childhood, and I believe sometimes used by drill-sergeants to enforce alertness in the training squad, depends upon a simple rule: the listener obeys the orders which are prefixed by the phrase "O'Grady says," but disobeys or ignores orders given without that prefix. Sooner or later, one "jumps to it," responding to the imperative tone, though the essential prefix has not been given. Amis uses the device of this exercise to explore the nature of authority, as we know it, and its relation to power.

[2] Kingsley Amis, from *A Look Round the Estate*.

Thus, after the first six lines we read from the poem the statement: "Authority is hollow; a thin cloak for the only naked face, power." But after the next three lines we read from the poem: "No. Authority is real; it genuinely exists to legitimize power, and not merely as rhetorical subterfuge." The next three lines say: "But since we have lost any confidence (it would have to be a religious or metaphysical confidence) that we can locate the one source of genuine authority in the world, it is as if there were no one such source but many." But, the poem goes on, this would not matter if the several sources were agreed to be objectively real. But we cannot agree or believe that this is the case, and a subjectively arrived at authority is equivalent to arbitrary power. The last three lines of the poem suggest that the answer to the conundrum is to acknowledge that the source of authority is human (some men have it, others haven't), but that this does not make it any less real. Indeed, the last four words—"Or so O'Grady says"—may be taken to mean that the location of authority in some men rather than in others may in fact have a divine or metaphysical sanction.

Amis was not alone among British poets of the 1950s in concerning himself with such matters. Here are the first three stanzas of a poem of my own which I wrote in 1953, called "Creon's Mouse":

> Creon, I think, could never kill a mouse
> When once that dangerous girl was put away,
> Shut up unbridled in her rocky house,
> Colossal nerve denied the light of day.
>
> Now Europe's hero, the humaner King
> Who hates himself, is humanised by shame,
> Is he a curbed or a corroded spring?
> A will that's bent, or buckled? Tense, or tame?
>
> If too much daring brought (he thought) the war,
> When that was over nothing else would serve
> But no one must be daring any more,
> A self-induced and stubborn loss of nerve.

This poem was seriously meant, and much of it I still subscribe to. A loss of nerve is what has saved us time and again in the years since 1953. It was what averted world war over Budapest in 1956, as also in 1968 over Prague, in which latest case it was in fact, and rightly, taken for granted. On the other side of the balance, an alarming recovery of nerve, "too much daring," was what took Britain into the Suez crisis and America into Vietnam. But I ask myself now, as apparently I didn't in 1953, "How much daring is too much?" What I didn't envisage then, which there is no excuse for not envisaging now, is that there would be people who would think it too daring of Creon to be a king at all, however self-limited and vowed to consultation and compromise. It is possible, I now have to realize, to think that it is audacious presumption for a man to get into any position of authority over his fellows, to take on any kind of institutionalized responsibility for directing them.

If I am challenged on this, I can point, for instance, to a letter which appeared in *The Listener* in 1968. Headed "End of the anti-university," the letter declared that that venture ran aground on precisely this rock. Mr. John Rowley, the writer of the letter, expostulated with his ex-colleagues in the anti-university: "But you need a 'place' and an 'organization' within it, however small and flexible, that is recognisable by all. Nobody seemed to be able to accept this. It meant an organization and that meant 'power,' which was anathema." Even at that point, Mr. Rowley said, the anti-university might have been saved if "some reluctant capitalist" had written a check; but this was impossible because "we are unable to tell him who to send it to." The difficulty, one would have thought, could have been foreseen. But apparently not. The anti-university was full of Antigones, not a Creon among them; and no one would take, or could be given, the authority to receive a check on behalf of the rest. For that would have been to acknowledge that the anti-university had been instituted and was therefore (insupportable word) an institution. When people behave like this, Creon's nerve has been buckled indeed.

Other people in 1968 were reading political lessons out of Soph-

ocles' *Antigone*. Conor Cruise O'Brien, writing in the same issue of
The Listener in which John Rowley's letter appeared, reminded us
that Antigone had a sister, Ismene, who resented Creon's order but
would not flout it; and he applied the situation between Creon
and Antigone and Ismene to the disturbance then occupying the
headlines in the news from Northern Ireland:

> There are many, even among the victims of the present conditions,
> who feel that the price of change would be too high, the spiritual
> children of Ismene are more numerous than those of Antigone, in
> Ulster as elsewhere. And their arguments, as always, are reason-
> able. The disabilities of Catholics in Northern Ireland are real,
> but not overwhelmingly oppressive; is their removal really worth
> attaining at the risk of precipitating riots, explosions, pogroms,
> murder? Thus Ismene. But Antigone will not heed such calcula-
> tions: she is an ethical and religious force, an uncompromising
> element in our being, as dangerous in her way as Creon, whom she
> perpetually challenges and provokes.

My sympathies have always been with Ismene, and they are even
more fervently with her in view of what has happened in Northern
Ireland since 1968. I have always thought that she had more reason to lose patience with Antigone than ever Creon had, though
neither Sophocles nor his commentators seem to have thought so.
Creon and Antigone understand each other rather well, they have
a great deal in common, more than either of them has with unheroic, painfully reasonable Ismene. So it is no surprise if Amis
has played Antigone in his time. As he did, I think, in a poem of
his called "Masters," which must have been written about the
same time as my "Creon's Mouse":

> That horse whose rider fears to jump will fall,
> Riflemen miss if orders sound unsure;
> They only are secure who seem secure;
>   Who lose their voice, lose all.
>
> Those whom heredity or guns have made
> Masters, must show it by a common speech;

Expected words in the same tone from each
    Will always be obeyed.

Likewise with stance, with gestures, and with face;
No more than mouth need move when words are said,
No more than hand to strike, or point ahead;
    Like slaves, limbs learn their place.

In triumph as in mutiny unmoved,
These make their public act their private good,
Their words in lounge or courtroom understood,
    But themselves never loved.

The eyes that will not look, the twitching cheek,
The hands that sketch what mouth would fear to own,
These only make us known, and we are known
    Only as we are weak:

By yielding mastery the will is freed,
For it is by surrender that we live,
And we are taken if we wish to give,
    Are needed if we need.[3]

I think this is an enviably well-written poem until the last stanza,
where the cadence smooths itself out with disconcerting slickness.
And not just the cadence, surely. For what follows if we take the
argument seriously and try to follow it through? Surely one thing
that might follow, one moral we might draw, is to act like Mr.
Rowley's anti-university colleagues. For if the only way to be
known and loved is not to act or speak with authority, then
shouldn't we at all costs refuse authority and neither sign nor receive checks on anyone's behalf? Always be in the Opposition,
never in the Government? Always refuse office? There is nothing
else that Antigone can do, if she is to remain Antigone.

   The interesting thing about Amis's poem is that his Antigone
refuses above all the supposed loneliness of office. In Sophocles'
play Antigone is the intransigent individual, a loner. But the An-

---

[3] Kingsley Amis, "Masters," from A Look Round the Estate.

tigones that tangle with the police on or off campus, or in the streets of Derry and London, are always in the plural, and think of themselves thus, as the speaker of "Masters" does. The price that our Antigones won't pay in order to take authority is the price of detachment from the collective. Of course, mass action is the only weapon they have. But their slogans and rallying cries, and their cooler statements also, make it clear that for most of them identification with the mass isn't just a strategic necessity but an emotional need, as witness their remarkable jumpiness about any allegations of a personality cult surrounding any of their leaders. Sophocles' Antigone could not be a social democrat; our Antigones are.

Conor Cruise O'Brien insists that Creon and Antigone and Ismene are universal types, or at least that the Creon-stance, the Antigone-stance, the Ismene-stance are constants of political action, in any place at any time. Doubtless this is right. Nikita Creon loses his nerve in the Cuban missile crisis, as Uncle Sam Creon loses his nerve over Budapest in 1956, as alas he doesn't lose it over Vietnam. But when we think that Russian Antigones are called Larisa Daniel and Pavel Litvinov, we are forced to remember how circumstances alter cases. There is nothing disingenuous nor hypocritical about admiring the Antigone-stance in certain situations and in certain societies, while deploring it in others. If Communism is not monolithic, neither is "protest." So the British Antigone can be seen and judged only if we separate her from Antigones elsewhere; she belongs and is to be understood only in the context of British society.

Amis's name for Antigone is "Lefty." Amis describes "the lefty" in one of his best poems, "After Goliath," which one can think of as "After Creon." In the poem, David, having laid the giant out cold, exults briefly over Goliath's adherents:

> Aldermen, adjutants, aunts,
> Administrators of grants,
> Assurance-men, auctioneers,
> Advisers about careers,

—all Creon types, of the sort hilariously pilloried in Amis's novels, *Lucky Jim* and *That Uncertain Feeling*. Lucky Dave then
pauses:

> But such an auspicious debut
> Was a little too good to be true,
> Our victor sensed; the applause
> From those who supported his cause
> Sounded shrill and excessive now,
> And who were they, anyhow?
> Academics, actors who lecture,
> Apostles of architecture,
> Ancient-gods-of-the-abdomen men,
> Angst-pushers, adherents of Zen,
> Alastors, Austenites, A-test
> Abolishers—even the straightest
> Of issues looks pretty oblique
> When a movement turns into a clique,
> The conqueror mused, as he stopped
> By the sword his opponent had dropped:
> Trophy, or means of attack
> On the rapturous crowd at his back?[4]

And in the years since, we have seen how Amis the giant killer
settled that last question: the weapon of his fame, wrenched from
the giant Establishment, has been turned on those who most applauded that assault. A sword taken from Creon has been used
against Antigone. And, allowing for the comic-dramatic convention of the poem (the catalogue gets more vehement and more
random as David's exasperation mounts), it is plain who Amis's
Antigone is: she is the British intelligentsia. If he calls her "Lefty,"
this is because the British intelligentsia has virtually no right wing
at all. Indeed, the delayed result of Fascism and of the Second
World War has been to taint or smear the whole right wing of
the political spectrum in England, so that for the most part the
range of permissible and expressible political attitudes in Britain
since 1945 has run only from the center to the left. Thus, any talk
of the Labour party or the Conservative party can only muddle

[4] Kingsley Amis, "After Goliath," from A *Look Round the Estate*.

the issue. And it is an issue too important to be muddled; nothing less than: what is an intelligentsia? Or what has it come to be in British society? What are the social privileges and obligations of an intelligentsia, and are these the privileges it enjoys, and the obligations it honors, in Britain today?

But we sometimes find it said that there is no such thing as a British intelligentsia, and that Britain is the poorer for the lack of it. When this view is expressed in academic circles, it is usually the preamble to a stirring call to university teachers to abandon the view of their function which Matthew Arnold had articulated for them. In the words of one exponent of this point of view, the professors must "abandon the status of Arnoldian defenders of culture," and "accept the distortions and special pleadings . . . involved in any attempt to make the past genuinely available to the present." According to the same authority, the British intellectuals must on the contrary "accept their role . . . as Sartre has accepted it in his brilliant and polemical literary studies." But of course no one who has been involved in recent disturbances on British campuses—for instance at the University of Essex in 1968, when Sartre, that eagle eye in its Paris aerie, intervened impudently by telegram—can doubt that we already have in England a politically conscious intellectual class in principled opposition to the national society, and ready on that principle to purvey "distortions and special pleadings" to the nation's student youth.

Surely, not only does Britain have in this deplorable sense an intelligentsia; it has had one for a long time, perhaps forty years, from just about the time in fact when Thomas Hardy died. All through that time, to be a British intellectual and yet not a socialist has meant swimming against the tide. What was new in the 1960s was the election to office of a socialist government which disappointed the hopes of most of the left-wing intellectuals who had helped to get it elected. But even if the Wilson government had chalked up a better record, the British intelligentsia would still have deserted it. For an intelligentsia, being on this showing a perpetual opposition, cannot be other than irresponsible. Like Antigone, it cannot afford ever to be responsible for the consequences of the actions it has demanded. And so it seems that any socialist government in Britain, however effective and honorable it might be, will always be disowned by the socialist intelligentsia of Britain, which will always move to the left so as to resume its oppositionist role.

Thus, one asks for an intelligentsia in the sense of a perpetual opposition only if one assumes intellectuals have a right to be politically irresponsible. As an intellectual myself I have never understood why any society should be expected to recognize that right, or be reproached for not conceding it. Czarist Russia, the society in which the concept of an intelligentsia was generated, never recognized nor conceded that right; nor did the Russian intelligentsia expect that it should.

Thus, when Isaiah Berlin argues that there is not a British intelligentsia, he means something quite different from what I have just been describing, and something altogether more acceptable. When Isaiah Berlin says that Britain has not and cannot have an intelligentsia, he means that British intellectuals have not earned, and cannot claim, the right to that privileged irresponsibility which the Russian intelligentsia could justly claim, not from Czarist society but, as it were, before posterity. If a society is so repressive that it will not let its intellectuals exercise any political responsibility at all, not even the responsibility that is incurred by openly debating political alternatives in the public prints, it forfeits its right to require its intellectuals to be responsible. Americans, in particular black Americans, are currently asking themselves whether American society is repressive enough (in more devious ways than were known to Czarist Russia), to justify them in taking or advocating politically irresponsible action. But only a lunatic fringe believes that British society is, or has been for at least a hundred years, repressive enough to give the British intellectual that justification. Yet there clearly is in Britain a class of people who assume and act upon this right which they have not earned, a body of educated persons who demand and act upon the right to be politically irresponsible; Antigones whose "colossal nerve" becomes more impudent wherever Creon's nerve is first bent and then broken. These are the people whose type is the Lefty as Amis defines him: "an intellectually disreputable and morally desensitized person."

How has it come about that British society not only tolerates such an intelligentsia (for that is what any democratic society has to do), but applauds it and is proud of it? No democratic society has yet found a way to restrict the influence that such people exert, and perhaps within a democracy no way can be found. But British society, so far from wishing to curtail the influence, encourages its intelligentsia and rewards it. In many areas of the national life it has sometimes seemed as if proven irresponsibility was the surest qualification for positions of responsibility and influence. It is foolish to start gobbling and hectoring about conspiracies and self-perpetuating cliques. The answer must be looked for somewhere else. I propose that the Antigones are so powerful in Britain because there are virtually no Creons left, and precious few Ismenes. Amis's Lefty gets his own way so often because he has us half converted before he starts. Those who should play Creon's role, or Ismene's, and conceive themselves to be doing so, believe in their hearts that Antigone is right. Lefty turns out to have involuntary sleepwalking allies in the most unlikely places. The poet who wrote "Masters" was such an involuntary accomplice, so I have suggested; and the poet who wrote "Creon's Mouse" was another. Yet another is the author of *The Hobbit* and *The Lord of the Rings*. And he is a specially instructive case.

For all we know, J. R. R. Tolkien may be a Labour voter. On the face of it, nothing seems much less likely. A Roman Catholic born in South Africa who has spent nearly all his professional life as fellow of an Oxford college, specializing in Old English—nothing could be much farther from the Lefty stereotype, or from the type of the British intelligentsia as I have tried to define it. (For to be a scholar does not automatically put you in the intelligentsia, nor does being a poet, a sculptor, or a painter put you there—but that is another argument). Yet I read *The Lord of the Rings* as a parable of authority, a parable pointing in one direction—towards the conviction that authority in public matters, because it is always spiritually perilous to the person it is vested in, can be and ought to be resisted and refused by anyone who wants to live humanely. And this is the conviction that the anti-university was based on; it is Antigone's conviction.

The Lord of the Rings is one of the most surprising products of British literature since 1945, and one of the most serious. Edmund Wilson's attack on the book, though it hearteningly insisted on the obvious—for instance that Tolkien's prose is as undistinguished as his verse—quite fails to account for the seriousness of the undertaking, for the pressure that drove the author through these thousand or more pages, as it has driven many readers (this reader among them) to follow through the same pages eagerly. The avidity with which *The Lord of the Rings* is read, the appeal of it and the loyalty it evokes among admirers—these are self-evident facts which cannot be explained convincingly by talk of frivolity and escapism.

At first sight there seems an obvious solution: the book answers to a hunger for the heroic. And to some degree this must be true; *The Lord of the Rings* is a grown-up's *Superman*. But the driving force of the book is unheroic, even antiheroic. The logic of the plot (which is very logical and tidy, not at all like medieval romance) is quite unequivocal; heroes are not to be trusted, only antiheroes. The heroes have the style of authority. They are always looking "stern" or "grave." And so Tolkien's narrative seems to contain many portentous images of civic authority taken and exercised—for instance, by Gandalf the wizard, and Aragorn the lost king who comes into his own. But though these heroes have the style of authority, they never have the fact of power. Tolkien asks us to admire them precisely because, when they are offered power, Gandalf and Aragorn refuse it. The villains are those, like another wizard, Saruman, who when they see a chance of power to back their authority, attempt to take it. And the contrast between Gandalf and Saruman is particularly interesting, because in the world that Tolkien has made the wizards are intellectuals. They are superhuman, however; and so, really, is Aragorn. He is called a man, but he is of superhuman mould, with an "elfish" admixture, and he lives much longer than normal men. Indeed the point of leverage for the whole of Tolkien's creation is an assumption the sourness of which is surprisingly little noticed, still less resented—the assumption that the hobbits, who are less than human, are the only beings in Tolkien's world that a human reader can, as we say, "identify with." We are forced to go along with this assumption because of the language that is put in the mouths of the hobbits, as contrasted with the more elevated and literary language that is spoken by everyone else. Though the language that the hobbits speak is not convincingly the language which the common Englishman does use (and sometimes, as in the case of the loyal servitor, Samwise, is quite embarrassingly wide of that mark), it is plainly meant to be so, and we register it as at least nearer to live spoken English than the archaic and rhetorical language given to all others.

What the narrative says is that neither Gandalf nor Aragorn can be trusted with the power of the magical Ring—a power which on the contrary can be entrusted safely only to the hobbit, Frodo. The idealistic and devotedly heroic capacities of men cannot be trusted with power; power can safely be invested (and even so not with complete safety, for even Frodo is tempted and falls, right at the end) only in those "halfling" men who, lost in a sleep of modestly sensual gratification, can rise to idealism only reluctantly and mistrustfully under the pressure of outrageous events, who behave heroically as it were in spite of themselves and to their own surprise, without premeditation. Thus the whole vast work tends to one end—to the elevation of the common man, of the private soldier over his officers and the schoolboy over his schoolmasters, of the sensual man over the intellectual, and of the spiritually lazy man over the spiritually exacting and ambitious. This is "the Dunkirk spirit," or "Theirs not to reason why":

> "Still we shall have to try," said Frodo. "It's no worse than I expected. I never hoped to get across. I can't see any hope of it now. But I've still got to do the best I can. . . ."[5]

[5] J. R. R. Tolkien, *The Return of the King*, Book VI, ch. II., *The Lord of the Rings*, Part III (Boston, 1956).

Although no hobbit can be imagined as fornicating, an American admirer of *The Lord of the Rings* got the message when he was moved to "memories of War, when unlettered, fornicating, foul-mouthed Tommies were heroes, pure and simple, on occasion. . ."

When a narrative calls up images so charged with sentiment as the fornicating Tommy and the Dunkirk beaches, anyone who carps at it has to be ready for trouble. So it is prudent to say that these images are charged for me too. A work of literature that calls them up, not explicitly but I think insistently, is Edwin Muir's poem, "The Combat," which in my opinion grasps more austerely than Tolkien everything in Tolkien's vision that can be made true and moving.

Amis's "Masters" is nearer to *The Lord of the Rings* than to "The Combat." All the same there are differences between Amis's concerns in his poem, and Tolkien's in his romance; differences that are important and also troublesome. They have to do with the difference between authority and power. Amis's poem is entirely concerned with authority, and in fact with the *style* of authority—with whatever it is in some sorts of behavior that makes such behavior authoritative. Tolkien is concerned with this, but he is also concerned with power. Gandalf and Aragorn have authority without power; and this, it seems, is all right. Frodo the hobbit has power without authority; and it seems that this is all right too. What is not all right, in Tolkien's scheme of things, is to be like Saruman the wicked wizard who wants power *and* authority, both at the same time, the one to back the other. Creon and even Ismene would find this hard to understand. And so do I. Power without authority, unauthorized power, is the power of the gangster. Authority without power, impotent authority, is the authority of the figurehead, the merely nominal head of state. But this is not the worst of it. If, as Amis does explicitly and Tolkien by implication, you identify authority with *style* ("They only are secure who seem secure"), then power without authority means power where we least expect it, power that is exerted upon us without manifesting itself: the power, for instance, of the advertiser and the media-manipulator—power which is all the more dangerous for not having any of the external marks by which we might recognize it, a power which operates under wraps or under the mask of the entertainer and the discreet or fawning servant. And authority without power, when authority is identified with style, becomes the magnetic or hypnotic authority of the great performer and the charismatic leader, the authority of a Hitler, whose authority *is* his power, and a very great power indeed. This authority is personal; it is conceded, and the power of it is exerted, in every classroom of any university or anti-university. "Your personal authority as a good teacher is unalienable; why do you need to have it registered in a title like Professor, and in privileges that go with that title?" Thus the campus rebels, speaking in the very accent of Antigone, and of J.R.R. Tolkien too. They do not understand, or they do not believe us, if we reply: "Because power that is authorized, and is seen to be authorized, is the only sort of power that can be controlled and allowed for and if necessary guarded against—by the man who wields it, but also and more urgently by those he wields it over, who may suffer by it."

Tolkien, it is well known, is far more popular with American youth than with British; and among radicals and dissidents as much as with the squares. The manager of the Berkeley campus bookstore told the *New York Times* (January 15, 1967), "This is more than a campus craze. It's like a drug dream." A vision so British as *The Lord of the Rings* cannot help but be distorted in the enthusiastic imagination of an American sophomore; and so one is sympathetic as well as amused, reading of Tolkien's distaste for things like the campaign buttons reading, "SUPPORT YOUR LOCAL HOBBIT" or "GO, GO, GANDALF." All the same, an editor for the American publishers of Tolkien in paperback was obviously in the right when he told the *New York Times*, "Young people today are interested in power and they are interested in working out the conflict of good and evil. Here it is worked out for them." It is indeed; perhaps perversely, but certainly with impressive consistency. Antigone is right to be grateful. And although American campus rebels are very different from the British rebels, it's reasonable to think that when they cry "Pigs!" at the representatives of authority on and off campus they, like their British counter-parts, are conceiving of a society from which authority shall seem to have vanished, where at any given moment overt authority shall be vested in no one at all. *The Lord of the Rings* endorses such hopes, and feeds them.

William Ready, who wrote *The Tolkien Relation*, speaks for a quite different section of Tolkien's American public. He is irri-tated and embarrassed by "the children and those who cherish simplicity, the wooden-beads-and-sandals set, in whom he [Tol-kien] has aroused enthusiasm. . ." And he admits, in some be-wilderment, "This is a surprising cult, this campus trend, because Tolkien is all conservative, traditional and rigid. . ." But, of course, no British reader need be bewildered. The Dunkirk spirit brings a lump to a Tory throat as soon as a cheer from a Labour confer-ence; Antigone is as ready to sprinkle regretful dust on the graves of our war dead as Creon is to deliver an oration over them. And British society, in entrusting itself ever since 1939 to the principle that has been called "a lot of weak government," has come per-haps as near as any society can to making itself into a society from which overt authority shall be absent; that is to say, just the sort of society which *The Lord of the Rings* incites us to realize.

For in practice a social organization based on the conviction that no man can be trusted with authority has to take the form of government by committee; and thus *The Lord of the Rings* can figure as an elaborate apology for the rule by bureaucracy which Britain has invited and endured for the last thirty years, under coalition and Conservative governments as well as under Labour. The committees have the authority. As for the power, that is with the advertisers and the commentators and the trend-setters, and with those members of committees—ministers, professors of eco-nomics, vice-chancellors, trades-union leaders, others—who hurry from the committee rooms to the T.V. studios.

They are all Antigones really; Creon's is such a thankless role in modern Britain that there is no one left to play it with convic-tion.

This is what Amis says in a poem called "Autobiographical

Fragment," which in its angry irony expresses an altogether more sympathetic attitude towards the authoritarian personality than had appeared in "Masters."

When I lived down in Devonshire
    The callers at my cottage
Were Constant Angst, the art critic,
    And old Major Courage.

Angst always brought me something nice
    To get in my good graces:
A quilt, a roll of cotton-wool,
    A pair of dark glasses.

He tore up all my unpaid bills,
    Went and got my slippers,
Took the telephone off its hook
    And bolted up the shutters.

We smoked and chatted by the fire,
    Sometimes just nodding;
His charming presence made it right
    To sit and do nothing.

But then—those awful afternoons
    I walked out with the Major!
I ran up hills, down streams, through briars;
    It was sheer blue murder.

Trim in his boots, riding-breeches
    And threadbare Norfolk jacket,
He watched me frowning, bawled commands
    To work hard and enjoy it.

I asked him once why I was there,
    Except to get all dirty;
He tugged his grey moustache and snapped:
    "Young man, it's your duty."

What duty's served by pointless, mad
    Climbing and crawling?
I tell you I was thankful when
    The old bore stopped calling.[6]

[6] Kingsley Amis, "Autobiographical Fragment," *A Case of Samples* (London, 1957).

Though Constant Angst back in 1956 represented irresponsible withdrawal from social concerns (he takes the telephone off the hook) rather than irresponsible intervention in them, his name is plainly Lefty, just as the Major (who has already "stopped calling") is Creon before his nerve was broken. For "the old bore" is surely a phrase that is meant to reflect back discreditably on the speaker. Such uneasily retrospective admiration for the vanished authoritarian figure is to be found in other writings of the late '50s, notably in the plays of John Osborne. One of Osborne's unattractive heroes complains, in an excuse which has been much quoted, that there are no causes left to die for. But Amis's poem suggests that it is not so much a matter of having no International Brigade to enlist in, as of having no Captain Tom Wintringham to advance behind—and equally no Orde Wingate to obey, no Captain Sherwood of the Royal Navy, above all no Churchill. I find Amis's diagnosis more plausible, because less self-congratulating, than Osborne's.

The virtues of Amis's writing in "Autobiographical Fragment" are those of Robert Graves at his best. The dry unshadowed silhouette of the Gravesian emblematic fable is also what pleases and carries conviction in "After Goliath." But in Amis's poems since 1957 "After Goliath" stands alone; no Gravesian virtues redeem any other poem in A Look Round the Estate, which is subtitled "Poems 1957-1967." This collection is deplorable; and if we are still looking in our poets for the presence of Hardy, we cannot be happy to think we catch a glimpse of him in the shrill and sentimental blasphemies of a poem called "New Approach Needed":

> . . . People have suffered worse
> And more durable wrongs
> Than you did on that cross
> (I know—you won't get me
> Up on one of those things),
> Without sure prospect of
> Ascending good as new

> On the third day, without
> "I die, but man shall live"
> As a nice cheering thought. . .[7]

However, it is not Hardy's remonstrances against his Creator—
thin and brittle stuff as those Hardy poems are—which lie behind
such an excess as this. The figure in the shadows is the more ele-
gant blasphemer whom Amis has elsewhere honored in accomplished and frigid pastiche:

A.E.H.

> Flame the westward skies adorning
> Leaves no like on holt or hill;
> Sounds of battle joined at morning
> Wane and wander and are still,
>
> Past the standards rent and muddied,
> Past the careless heaps of slain,
> Stalks a redcoat who, unbloodied,
> Weeps with fury, not from pain.
>
> Wounded lads, when to renew them
> Death and surgeons cross the shade,
> Still their cries, hug darkness to them;
> All at last in sleep are laid.
>
> All save one, who nightlong curses
> Wounds imagined more than seen,
> Who in level tones rehearses
> What the fact of wounds must mean.[8]

Loose lips and tight lips tell the same story: the Yahoo bluster of
the one, the professorial curtness of the other, provoke in us (admiringly, if all works out right) the tone which is insistently present to just the degree that it is conspicuously choked back or
shouted down—the tone of whining self-pity. For Housman's

[7] Amis, "New Approach Needed," *A Look Round the Estate*.
[8] Amis, "A.E.H.," *A Look Round the Estate*.

Spirit of Irony easily accommodates self-pity, whereas Hardy's
Spirit of Pity does not. (It is looking the other way).

It gives me no pleasure to write of Kingsley Amis in this way.
But anyone who thinks me unfair when I detect self-pity, ought to
turn to other pieces in A *Look Round the Estate*, like the dis-
tressingly explicit "A Chromatic Passing-Note." And there is more
to be said of the failure of A *Look Round the Estate*. For it cannot be coincidence that the only good poem in that collection,
"After Goliath," is also the only poem that is political. As a polemicist Amis has been politically active of recent years—notably, and
valuably, in the struggle (doubtless foredoomed, but a fight that
must be fought) to maintain a modicum of authority for at least
one representative figure in one situation, that is to say, for the
teacher in his schoolroom. Yet this concern for authority, which
was the nerve of the best of Amis's earlier poems, has of late ex-
pended itself entirely in such polemic and public action, leaving
the poems to expostulate not with public servants like "aldermen"
and "administrators of grants," but only with the figure of straw
that atheists label "God." Of course Amis's master had gone the
same way long before; Graves, once the social historian of *The
Long Week-End*, withdrew forty years ago to Majorca and has
since found a retreat even more securely insulated from British
social and political realities—the mythological Never-Never Lands
ruled over by goddesses, white and black, where lately he seems to
have been joined in mumbo-jumbo by Ted Hughes.[9] Amis is too
responsible to take that way out. And if we want to seduce him
from a Housmanesque allegiance to another more sturdy and com-
prehensively humane, we may tempt him by citing Hardy at his
most liberal and least socialist, least "Lefty":

> I find that my politics really are neither Tory nor radical. I may
> be called an intrinsicalist. I am against privilege derived from ac-
> cident of any kind, and am therefore equally opposed to aristo-
> cratic privilege and democratic privilege. (By the latter I mean the
> arrogant assumption that the only labour is hand-labour—a worse

9 Ted Hughes, in *The London Magazine* (January 1971), p. 6.

arrogance than that of the aristocrat,—the taxing of the worthy to help those masses of the population—who will not help themselves when they might, etc.) Opportunity should be equal for all, but those who will not avail themselves of it should be cared for merely —not be a burden to, nor the rulers over, those who do avail themselves thereof.[10]

In these comments of 1888 there speaks plainly the self-made man, the hero (or the martyr) of self-help. But they take on a more generally applicable resonance when set beside some observations of three years before:

History is rather a stream than a tree. There is nothing organic in its shape, nothing systematic in its development. It flows on like a thunderstorm-rill by a road side; now a straw turns it this way, now a tiny barrier of sand that. The offhand decision of some commonplace mind high in office at a critical moment influences the course of events for a hundred years. Consider the evenings at Lord Carnarvon's, and the intensely average conversation on politics held there by average men who two or three weeks later were members of the Cabinet. A row of shopkeepers in Oxford Street taken just as they come would conduct the affairs of the nation as ably as these.

Thus, judging by bulk of effect, it becomes impossible to estimate the intrinsic value of ideas, acts, material things: we are forced to appraise them by the curves of their career. There were more beautiful women in Greece than Helen; but what of them?[11]

That last question—"more beautiful women in Greece than Helen; but what of them?"—is unanswerable in terms of the right-wing mythological politics of Pound or of Yeats. But it is no more answerable in terms of the historically determinist politics of Marx; for "judging by bulk of effect, it becomes impossible to estimate the intrinsic value of ideas, acts, material things," or, we must add, of persons—among whom, as Amis has bemusedly noticed, some have innate authority, whereas others haven't.

[10] *The Life of Thomas Hardy 1840-1928*, p. 204.
[11] *The Life of Thomas Hardy 1840-1928*, p. 172.

Amis has many years yet in which to redeem the calamity of *A Walk Round the Estate*. One way to do so would be to resume in his poems the investigation of the fact of authority, instead of letting his concern with it lead him, as a public figure, into excusing the inexcusable, for instance the presence of the Americans in Vietnam. Unless he or some one else does this, the British will have to concur in the saturnine analysis of *The Lord of the Rings*, and subscribe themselves, when all is said and done, not men but hobbits.

~5~

The Hawk's Eye

Since I must hold to the gradual in
this, as no revolution but a slow change
like the image of snow. The challenge is
not a moral excitement, but the expanse
  the continuing patience
  dilating into forms so
  much more than compact.[1]

If we were right to think that the unusual rigidity and intricacy of Hardy's meters and stanza patterns had something to do with the phase of Victorian culture which he lived through, that of heavy engineering, we shall not expect to find this characteristic transmitted to any of his successors. For we need not subscribe to the comically confident assertions of some authorities, who would have it that because our technology is now electronic, there is a sort of necessity for the poet to compose "by field"; but we may well feel that indeed the way in which Hardy rivets one verse line to another by clanging exact rhymes and builds up in this way a finely tooled metrical machine, is inappropriate to our sense of

---

[1] J. H. Prynne, "Moon Poem," from *The White Stones* (Lincoln, 1969). J. H. Prynne, born 1936, is Fellow of a Cambridge college. His publications are *Force of Circumstance & Other Poems* (London: Routledge & Kegan Paul, 1962); *Kitchen Poems* (London: Goliard, 1968); *Aristeas* (London: Ferry Press, 1969); *The White Stones* (Lincoln: Grosseteste Press, 1969); and *Brass* (London: Ferry Press, 1971).

what really conditions and keeps running the world in which we live now.

However, there is the exceptional case of John Betjeman. For in Betjeman's poetry we do find, in the decades since Hardy died, something approaching the rigidity and intricacy of Hardy's metrical procedures. If the particular model in some of Betjeman's poems is Kipling rather than Hardy, this does not alter our sense that in any case the forms are inappropriate to the historical circumstances in which the poet is using them, and indeed that Betjeman is in many instances attracted to them for just this reason; in other words, that there is an air of antiquarianism and connoisseurship which hangs heavily around many of Betjeman's poems which are most expert and intricate as metrical constructions.

Thus, I find Betjeman most successful and most moving when his writing least reminds me of anything one might find in Hardy or Kipling or another poet of their generation. This holds true even when the master that we hear Betjeman's poem allude to is a poet of an earlier generation yet, for instance Tennyson. The effect is more valuable still when Betjeman has asserted his independence of Hardy not just in his verse forms but also in what he chooses to say; for instance, when he is as straightforwardly and unaffectedly Christian as Hardy is atheist. One of Betjeman's most touching and valuable poems is one that qualifies on both these counts, "Sunday Afternoon Service in St. Enodoc's Church, Cornwall." This poem, in skillful but unobtrusive and unambitious blank verse, is too long to quote in full; this is a pity, because a great deal of the impressiveness of the poem depends upon the way in which it sustains itself through easy modulations of tone and feeling. But something of the sure and fine transitions can be seen even in an excerpt:

> Where deep cliffs loom enormous, where cascade
> Mesembryanthemum and stone-crop down,
> Where the gull looks no larger than a lark
> Hung midway twixt the cliff-top and the sand,
> Sun-shadowed valleys roll along the sea.
> Forced by the backwash, see the nearest wave

Rise to a wall of huge, translucent green
And crumble into spray along the top
Blown seaward by the land-breeze. Now she breaks
And in an arch of thunder plunges down
To burst and tumble, foam on top of foam,
Criss-crossing, baffled, sucked and shot again,
A waterfall of whiteness, down a rock,
Without a source but roller's furthest reach:
And tufts of sea-pink, high and dry for years,
Are flooded out of ledges, boulders seem
No bigger than a pebble washed about
In this tremendous tide. Oh kindly slate!
To give me shelter in this crevice dry.
Those shivering stalks of bent-grass, lucky plant,
Have better chance than I to last the storm.
Oh kindly slate of these unaltered cliffs,
Firm, barren substrate of our windy fields!
Oh lichened slate in walls, they knew your worth
Who raised you up to make this House of God.
What faith was his, that dim, that Cornish saint,
Small rushlight of a long-forgotten church,
Who lived with God on this unfriendly shore
Who knew He made the Atlantic and the stones
And destined seamen here to end their lives
Dashed on a rock, rolled over in the surf,
And not one hair forgotten. Now they lie
In centuries of sand beside the church.
Less pitiable are they than the corpse
Of a large golfer, only four weeks dead,
This sunlit and sea-distant afternoon.
"Praise ye the Lord!" and in another key
The Lord's name by harmonium be praised.
"The Second Evening and the Fourteenth Psalm."[2]

Even here of course the coy or quizzical allusions to past idioms,
Tennyson's and earlier, sink the poem away from us behind a glaze
of knowledgeability in the poet; and there will always be readers
to whom that sort of knowing play with one idiom poised against
another will seem antipathetic. However, there are many other

[2] John Betjeman, "Sunday Afternoon Service in St. Enodoc's Church, Cornwall," *John Betjeman's Collected Poems* (Boston, 1958, 2nd ed., 1962).

poets beside Betjeman, and poets who are much greater, who will by that token be beyond such a reader.

When W. H. Auden was introducing Betjeman to an American audience, in 1947, he faced the matter of this compulsion in Betjeman always to quiz his readers:

> I will content myself with asserting dogmatically that, this season, the man of good will will wear his heart up his sleeve, not on it. For better or worse, we who live in this age not only feel but are critically conscious of our emotions. . . and, in consequence, again for better or worse, a naive rhetoric, one that is not confessedly "theatrical," is now impossible in poetry. The honest manly style is today only suited to Iago.[3]

But this prophecy was no sooner uttered than events disproved it. In the years since 1947, on both sides of the Atlantic, naïve rhetorics and manly tones have been very much in evidence. The quizzical and evasive ironies which are favored by both Auden and Betjeman now seem to be a peculiarity of their age group, not a condition of "this age." In any case, in "Sunday Afternoon Service in St. Enodoc's Church, Cornwall," the reader is quizzed by the poet only from time to time, and then gently and with tact; the poet's eye (and therefore the reader's) is elsewhere—on the matter being contemplated, not on the relations of the poet-performer with his audience.

As much cannot be said, however, of poems in which Betjeman draws nearer to the Hardyesque. There is, to take a blatant example, a poem called "Dorset," which is an imitation of Hardy's "Friends Beyond":

> Light's abode, celestial Salem! Lamps of evening, smelling strong,
> Gleaming on the pitch-pine, waiting, almost empty evensong:
> From the aisles each window smiles on grave and grass and yew-
>   tree bough—
> While Tranter Reuben, Gordon Selfridge, Edna Best and
>   Thomas Hardy lie in Mellstock Churchyard now.[4]

[3] W. H. Auden, Introduction to *Slick But Not Streamlined. Selected Writings of John Betjeman* (New York, 1947).
[4] Betjeman, "Dorset," from the *Collected Poems.*

And a coy and maddening footnote by the author tells us that the names in the last line of this stanza and in the corresponding line of the two earlier stanzas—T. S. Eliot, H. G. Wells, Edith Sitwell, Mary Borden, Brian Howard, Harold Acton—are "put in not out of malice or satire but merely for their euphony." The self-conscious "tease" of performing the parody at all, compounded by the double-take to which this disingenuous footnote invites us, puffs such a dense vapor of self-consciousness about the poet's relationship to his readers that behind it the lineaments of the poem as in any way a considered utterance entirely disappear.

A much less obvious case, but one which in the end we have to regret more bitterly, is a poem called "The Heart of Thomas Hardy":

> The heart of Thomas Hardy flew out of Stinsford churchyard
> A little thumping fig, it rocketed over the elm trees.
> Lighter than air it flew straight to where its Creator
> Waited in golden nimbus, just as in eighteen sixty,
> Hardman and son of Brum had depicted Him in the chancel.
> Slowly out of the grass, slitting the mounds in the centre
> Riving apart the roots, rose the new covered corpses
> Tess and Jude and His Worship, various unmarried mothers,
> Woodmen, cutters of turf, adulterers, church restorers,
> Turning aside the stones thump on the upturned churchyard.
> Soaring over the elm trees slower than Thomas Hardy,
> Weighted down with a Conscience, now for the first time fleshly
> Taking form as a growth hung from the feet like a sponge-bag.
> There, in the heart of the nimbus, twittered the heart of Hardy
> There, on the edge of the nimbus, slowly revolved the corpses
> Radiating around the twittering heart of Hardy,
> Slowly started to turn in the light of their own Creator
> Died away in the night as frost will blacken a dahlia.[5]

The extremely difficult verse line, one sort of English hexameter, is handled here with something approaching Hardy's inventiveness and finesse in similarly ringing the changes upon rare and difficult metrical arrangements. One notes admiringly how fast the poem

[5] Betjeman, "The Heart of Thomas Hardy," from *Collected Poems*.

gathers speed, to take off with "rocketed" in the second line; and
how Betjeman uses the rapidity of spoken rather than written syntax, in a touch like the adverbial "thump" of line 10. And the
grotesque literalness of the image created, a myth rendered with
the effect of hallucination, can without self-evident foolishness,
and appropriately enough considering the subject, be described
as Dantesque. If for the first and even the second reading the direction of the poem, and the intention behind it, remain equiv-
ocal—is the poem a tribute to Hardy, or an attack on him?—we are
ready to believe that the ambiguity faithfully reflects the struggle
of emotions in a reverently believing poet when regarding the
spectacle of his loved and admired master who is infidel and blasphemer. In fact I take the poem to be a hyperbolical compliment
to Hardy, in that his fictional creations at least *start* to turn
around him, as the souls of God's creations turn around Him
continually in eternal adoration and love. Indeed we should have
to say that the admiration for Hardy and the pity for him are in
this poem adjusted one to the other most memorably, were it not
for a single betraying phrase—"various unmarried mothers." Everything else in the poem, certainly including the makers of the
Brummagem sacred furniture, if it is appropriate to the character
or the *persona* of John Betjeman, is appropriate no less to the
character and the historical circumstances of Thomas Hardy. The
image of the conscience made physically present, "hung from the
feet like a sponge-bag," is magnificent. But . . . "various unmarried mothers"! At that point in the poem, quite needlessly and
ruinously, there intrudes a flippantly knowing and heartless voice
out of some shallowly competitive conversation at a college high
table. The failure of nerve is lamentable and irredeemable: and
the chance of a more splendid compliment to Hardy than anyone
else is likely to pay has been irretrievably muffed and missed. This
is what happens when the cosmic irony with which, in Hardy or
Housman, the universe confronts man, becomes the evasive and
defensive irony with which the poet confronts the universe, including that part of the human universe which he envisages as his
readers.

If I propose that this sort of evasive obliquity in the poet's stance toward his audience was forced upon Betjeman by the inappropriately rigid forms which he adopted from Hardy, rather than from some psychological or social maladjustment in himself, I am giving him the benefit of the doubt. I am happy to do so, however; it is a sort of giving to which critics are not much prone. The point to be made is in any case one that does not depend upon this particular illustration, though this may enforce it. The rigidly intricate metrical and stanzaic arrangements of Hardy could be used, in the years after his death, only by poets who were willing or eager to stand obliquely to their audience. This is not the same as saying (what I do not believe) that the traditional accentual-syllabic meters of English have been self-evidently superseded by *vers libre*; it is a quality of curious tenacity in the handling and elaboration of those meters which seems to be appropriate to the generation of Hardy and Hopkins, Patmore and Kipling, but inappropriate to every generation since.

If this can be granted, it raises the possibility that the sort of verse style which I have called Hardyesque can survive into, and be detected in, verse writing which obeys none of the criteria—of symmetry, parallelism, and rigorous equivalence—which normally governed Hardy's own writing in verse. And in "Sunday Afternoon Service in St. Enodoc's Church, Cornwall," the play that Betjeman makes with Cornish slate suggests one way in which this may be true. For a parallel, there is an indifferent poem by Hardy, entitled "Green Slates (Penpethy)":

> It happened once, before the duller
>   Loomings of life defined them,
> I searched for slates of greenish colour
>   A quarry where men mined them;
>
> And saw, the while I peered around there,
>   In the quarry standing
> A form against the slate background there,
>   Of fairness eye-commanding.

And now, though fifty years have flown me,
   With all their dreams and duties,
And strange-pipped dice my hand has thrown me,
   And dust are all her beauties,

Green slates—seen high on roofs, or lower
   In waggon, truck, or lorry—
Cry out: "Our home was where you saw her
   Standing in the quarry!"

These slates, and more generally, the geological and topographical features of landscape which play such a major role in Hardy's poems particularly of bereavement, are among those images which Raymond Williams allows for, even as he argues that Hardy's vision is more precisely conditioned historically than most critics are willing to admit:

> It is also obvious that, in most rural landscapes, there are very old and often unaltered features, which sustain a quite different time scale. Hardy gives great importance to these, and this is not really surprising, when we consider his whole structure of feeling.[5]

Hardy's feeling for topography and locality, as somehow conditioning the human lives lived under their influence more powerfully than any theory available to him or to us can allow for, is something that can and does persist, as a tradition, quite athwart the evident discontinuities, between him and us, in the way that artistic form, and specifically poetic form, is conceived. The poet who wrote "Green Slates," or, in "The Going," "You were she who abode/By those red-veined rocks far West," or "Primaeval rocks form the road's steep border,/And much have they faced there, first and last,/Of the transitory in Earth's long order" ("At Castle Boterel"), is not outside the range of sympathy of a contemporary poet who responds with elation to the possibility of placing himself according to geological, rather than humanly historical, time:

[5] See Raymond Williams, "Thomas Hardy," in *The Critical Quarterly*, 6.4 (Winter 1964), pp. 341-51.

Age by default: in some way this must
be solved. The covenants that bind
into the rock, each to the other
are for this, for the argon dating
    by song as echo of the world.
    O it runs sweetly by, and prints over
    the heart; I am supremely happy,
the whole order set in this, the
proper guise, of a song. You can hear
the strains from so far off: withdrawn
    from every haunted place
    in its graveness, the responsive
    shift into the millions of years.
I am born back there, the plaintive chanting
under the Atlantic and the unison of forms.
It *may* all flow again if we suppress the
    breaks, as I long to do,
    at the far end of that distance
    and tidings of the land . . .[6]

And yet the author of these lines, J. H. Prynne, is a poet as vowed to the open-ended and diffusive forms of verse as Hardy was to the constrictive.

Though Prynne appears to have taken instruction from American practitioners of "composition by field," like Charles Olson and Edward Dorn, who share his and Hardy's concern with defining human beings by the topographical location which they occupy, he could also—and I would guess he did—take his bearings from a native source, that is to say, from Hardy. For certainly, Prynne's emphasis is frequently on patience, on lowering the sights, settling for limited objectives. And all of this side of what he says is as far as possible from the sanguine expansiveness of the American poets whom he has read and emulates. In "The Holy City," he writes:

Where we go is a loved side of the temple,
a place for repose, a concrete path.
There's no mystic moment involved: just

[6] Prynne, "The Wound, Day and Night," in *The White Stones*.

> that we are
> is how, each
> severally, we're
> carried into
> the wind which makes no decision and is
> a tide, not taken. I saw it
> and love is
> when, how &
> because we
> do: you
> could call it Ierusalem or feel it
> as you walk, even quite jauntily, over the grass.[7]

I take this to mean: love of others is a matter of recognizing their right to exist, and that comes about from accepting them and yourself in relation to elemental and uncaring presences like wind and sun. Similarly, Prynne has his own poem "against extremity":

> Finally it's trade that the deep changes
> work with, so that the lives are heavier,
> less to be moved from or blunted. The city
> is the language of transfer
>   to the human account. Here
>   the phrases shift, the years
>   are an acquiescence.
> This isn't a wild comment: there's no
> good in the brittle effort, to snap the pace
> into some more sudden glitter of light:
>   hold to this city or the slightly pale
>   walking, to a set rhythm of
>   the very slight hopefulness. That
> is less than patience, it's time or more clearly
> the sequence of years; a thickening in the words
> as the coins themselves wear thin and could
>   almost balance on the quick
>   ideal edge. The stirring is so
>   slight, the talk so stunned, the
> city warm in the air, it is a
> too steady shift and life as
> it's called is age and the merest impulse,

---

7 "The Holy City," in *The White Stones.*

                    called the city and the deep
                    blunting damage of hope.
                    That's where it is, now
              as the place to be left and the last
              change still in return: down there
              in the snow, too, the loyal city of man.[8]

The structuring principle of this poetry, which makes it difficult
(sometimes too difficult), is the unemphasized but radical demands it makes upon English etymologies, so that to follow the
logic we have to remember "trade" as meaning traffic, for instance
pedestrian traffic in the streets, also exchange and interchange, as
of current coin and current language in human as well as commer-
cial transactions and transfers. And though Hardy like any good
poet may go for his effects into that dimension of language, of
course his poetry does not work in that dimension at all so constantly as Prynne's does. Other differences between the two poets
are too obvious to be worth commenting on. And yet the sentiment on which Prynne's poem comes to rest is not far from one
that Hardy expresses, especially when he contemplates features of
topography. An example (in which the first line is unfortunate
self-parody), is "Yell'ham-Wood's Story," dated 1902:

                Coomb-Firtrees say that Life is a moan,
                        And Clyffe-hill Clump says "Yea!"
                But Yell'ham says a thing of its own:
                        It's not "Gray, gray
                        Is Life alway!"
                        That Yell'ham says,
                Nor that Life is for ends unknown.

                It says that Life would signify
                        A thwarted purposing:
                That we come to live, and are called to die.
                        Yes, that's the thing
                        In fall, in spring,
                        That Yell'ham says:—
                "Life offers—to deny!"

[8] "In the Long Run, To Be Stranded," in *The White Stones*. The poem is
given in full.

❧

If it still seems, as no doubt it does, that only special pleading can bridge the evident discrepancies between Hardy's way of writing and J.H. Prynne's, incredulity may be eased a little by considering as representative of the intervening generations a figure more substantial than John Betjeman; that is to say, Auden. Auden has more than once paid homage to Hardy as his own first master, though seldom without a faint air of condescension. Yet no one I think has yet succeeded in locating the Hardyesque contribution to Auden's subsequent styles and concerns; and where others have failed, I may be allowed to guess. Accordingly, I will guess that part of the continuing inheritance from Hardy in Auden's poetry is the importance for the later poet of topography, the frequency with which specific landscapes (particularly those of his native Pennine limestone) serve as the provocation for Auden's imagination, and the focus of some of his most delicate and feelingful writing. Introducing Betjeman's poems, Auden coined the words "topophil" and "topophilia" to characterize the sort of topographical poet that Betjeman is, and the sort of habit of mind which in Betjeman gets poetic expression. He remarked:

> Topophilia differs from the farmer's love of his home soil and the litterateur's fussy regional patriotism in that it is not possessive or limited to any one locality; the practiced topophil can operate in a district he has never visited before. On the other hand, it has little in common with nature-love. Wild or unhumanised nature holds no charms for the average topophil because it is lacking in history; (the exception which proves the rule is the geological topophil). At the same time, though history manifested by objects is essential, the quantity of the history and the quality of the object are irrelevant; a branch railroad is as valuable as a Roman wall, a new tudor teashop as interesting as a Gothic cathedral. America is so big, the countryside not actually under cultivation so wild, that the automobile is essential to movement. Topophilia, however, cannot survive at velocities greater than that of a somewhat rusty bicycle. (Hence, Betjeman's obsession with that vehicle.)[9]

[9] Auden, from his Introduction to *Slick But Not Streamlined: Selected Writings of John Betjemen* (New York, 1947).

Those last sentences look forward twenty years to "Prologue. The Birth of Architecture," where Auden tells John Bayley:

> From gallery-grave and the hunt of a wren-King
>   to Low Mass and trailer camp
> is hardly a tick by the carbon clock, but I
>   don't count that way nor do you:
> already it is millions of heartbeats ago
>   back to the Bicycle Age,
> before which is no *After* for me to measure,
>   just a still prehistoric *Once*.

And we may certainly reflect that in Hardy's poems as much as in Betjeman's the commonest and most favored vehicle is the bicycle. However, Auden declares, having defined the sort of topophil poet that he takes Betjeman to be: "It is one of my constant regrets that I am too short-sighted, too much of a Thinking Type, to attempt this sort of poetry, which requires a strongly visual imagination." And yet, however we may regard this deprecating modesty on Auden's part, it is plain that he has left himself a valuable niche in the parenthetical room he has left for "the geological topophil." For in Auden's poetry, from those early poems which make such ominous play with images of flooded mine shafts and abandoned mine workings, through to "In Praise of Limestone" and beyond, there is a steady concern with the stony bones of various landscapes. And this is something which Prynne has in common with Auden, as we shall see.

No one would maintain that Hardy lacked "a strongly visual imagination,' or, more generally and more pertinently, a capacity to occupy a particular scene or situation with all his senses alert. Descriptions like "Overlooking the River Stour" or "On Sturminster Foot-Bridge," or such magnificent presentations as "A Spellbound Palace" or "The Sheep Boy," spring at once to mind. And yet in Hardy's more ambitious poems, those which approach and achieve the condition of phantasmagoria, the poet is content to be impressionistic and use a broad brush. For instance, in "Wessex Heights" the different kinds of landscape comprised in Wessex—

its hills, its lowlands, and its plain—are rendered by an imagination
which has abstracted the main and determining features of each:

> There are some heights in Wessex, shaped as if by a kindly hand
> For thinking, dreaming, dying on, and at crises when I stand,
> Say, on Ingpen Beacon eastward, or on Wylls-Neck westwardly,
> I seem where I was before my birth, and after death may be. . . .
>
> I cannot go to the great grey Plain; there's a figure against the
>   moon,
> Nobody sees it but I, and it makes my breast beat out of tune. . .

The different kinds of landscape are adverted to in turn, chiefly
so as to bring out the sort of emotional and social life which each
of them seems to require of the speaker of the poem. And this is
precisely the interest, requiring the poet's imagination to abstract
and generalize, which we find for instance in Auden's "Bucolics."
It is almost as if each of Auden's long poems under this title—
"Mountains," "Lakes," "Islands," "Plains," "Streams"—were an
elaboration and development of a perception starkly indicated by
different stanzas in Hardy's poem, with the characteristic difference, however, that the deprecating category, "Bucolics," permits
or requires Auden to descend to moments of bumpkin bathos:
"Just reeling off their names is ever so comfy," or "Five minutes on
even the nicest mountain/Is awfully long."

Neither in Hardy nor in Auden is there any sign of that determination to render the particular scene, experience, or topic in
all its particularized quiddity which we find in Ruskin, in Hopkins's poems (and his theories of "inscape" and "instress"), and,
in the present day, in characteristic poems by Charles Tomlinson.
As for Prynne, he has a poem, "For a Quiet Day," in which he
appears to consider this way of encountering the nonhuman creation as he might have met it in Tomlinson, and firmly though
respectfully to reject it:

> There are some men that focus
> on the true intentness, as I know
> and wouldn't argue with: it is
> violent, the harp—I will not do it

though, and the time is
so gentle, in the shadow
that any youth might
sleep. But I will
not do it, with the gilded harp
and of all things, its pedals, for
the nice touch. As the curves too
are sometimes gentle, where we shall be
in the succession of
light, hope, the
evening
distracts: and it is always too
fine, too hopeless and will not let
the gentle course—by the chance
rise of a voice.
And if the intentness
is the more true, then
I want the gentler
course, where
the evening is more of what we are:
or the day as well—moist, casual,
broken by inflictions of touch. This
is the resting-place, out in the street.
That we are so, and
for the other thing
I will not do it, will
not; this is a quiet day.[10]

Though the extremes that are here being guarded against and
excluded include those which Tomlinson also has ruled out in
"Against Extremity," Prynne's poem exorcises also that Ruskinian
or Hopkinsian extreme of anguished perception to which Tomlinson is subject, to which indeed he seems to have vowed himself.
What Prynne most values would be broken by, would experience
as an infliction, the "nice" (the precisely and exactly discriminat-
ing) "touch." The "curves" which Prynne here holds before us as
the image of a longed-for civil and equable way of life and behavior, are embodied in his own sentences which, strung as they are
across his hesitant short lines, very frequently change direction in

[10] Prynne, "For a Quiet Day," in *The White Stones*.

mid-course. But, as other poems in *The White Stones* make clear, the curves are also—and even principally—those of a gently undulating countryside, its shallow contours ground down by glacial erosion during one or another ice age. An elaborate and beautiful poem by Prynne, "The Glacial Question Unsolved," seems to say this, among other things. In Hardy and Auden and Prynne alike the long temporal perspectives of geology induce a quietness which, though it is undermined by apprehension, seems like a liberation:

> So I am found on Ingpen Beacon, or on Wylls-Neck to the west,
> Or else on homely Bulbarrow, or little Pilsdon Crest,
> Where men have never cared to haunt, nor women have walked
>   with me,
> And ghosts then keep their distance; and I know some liberty.

However, the political implication or analogue is plain and dismaying. It is quietism, an impasse, inaction; as Prynne says elsewhere, in a passage which there seems to be no point in printing as verse: "Contentment or sceptical calm will produce instant death at the next jolt & intending suicides should carry a card at least exonerating the eventual bystanders. . ." Thus, if all these poets are scientific humanists (for neither in Prynne nor in Auden is the science of geology merely a source for illustrative metaphor), plainly what we have is scientific humanism at the end of its tether. Of course if it were in any other condition, we should rightly refuse to listen to it; and for that matter Jeremy Prynne is not being listened to in any case.

Meanwhile, the geological or geographical time scale at least serves to reveal the absurdity of all forms of Utopian revolution:

>   . . . what is anyone waiting
> *for*, either resigned or nervous or frantic from
> time to time? Various forms dodge through
> the margins of a livelihood, but so much talk
> about the underground is silly when it would re-
> quire a constant effort to keep below the surface,
> when almost everything is exactly that, the
> mirror of a would-be alien who won't see how

much he is at home. In consequence also the
idea of change is briskly seasonal, it's too cold
& thus the scout-camp idea of revolution stands
in temporary composure, waiting for spring. All
forms of delay help this farce, that our restrictions
are temporary & that the noble fiction is to have
a few good moments, which represent what we know
ought to be ours. Ought to be, that makes me
wince with facetiousness: we/you/they, all the
pronouns by now know how to make a sentence
work with *ought to*, and the stoic at least saves
himself that extremity of false vigilance.[11]

The wince of exasperation makes for good impatient prose, if not
for anything that we can usefully call verse.

Already in 1939 Cleanth Brooks decided that "the central im-
pulse of Auden's poetry" could be located in some early verses
which Brooks quoted:

> And all emotions to expression came,
> Recovering the archaic imagery:
> The longed for assurance takes the form
>
> Of a hawk's vertical stooping from the sky;
> These tears, salt for a disobedient dream,
> The lunatic agitation of the sea;
>
> While this despair with hardened eyeballs cries
> "A Golden Age, a Silver . . . rather this,
> Massive and taciturn years, the Age of Ice."

Brooks commented:

Auden's surest triumphs represent a recovery of the archaic imagery—fells, scarps overhung by kestrels, the becks with their pot-
holes left by the receding glaciers of the age of ice. His dominant
contrast is the contrast between this scene and the modern age of
ice: foundries with their fires cold, flooded coal-mines, silted harbours—the debris of the new ice age. The advent of the new age of
ice, a "polar peril," supplies the background for his finest poetry.[12]

[11] "Questions for the Time Being," from *The White Stones* (Lincoln, 1969).
[12] Cleanth Brooks, *Modern Poetry and the Tradition* (Chapel Hill, 1939);
Reprinted in *Auden: A Collection of Critical Essays*, ed. by M. K. Spears
(Englewood Cliffs, 1964), pp. 17-18.

So much has happened to Auden in the past thirty years that no
doubt Cleanth Brooks would not hold to the same confident
judgment now, or not without qualifications. What is striking is
that the same description—of humankind seen as inhabiting a
span between an ice age long past and another which is imminent
—fits exactly Prynne's collection *The White Stones*, as well as particular pieces in that connection, such as "The Glacial Question,
Unsolved."

The landscapes of those early poems by Auden are so insistently
those of Craven in the Yorkshire Pennines that one would not
think of connecting them with the chalk landscapes of Hardy's
Wessex.[13] Yet we have Auden's own word for it that such a connection exists. Looking back from 1940 at the period of his youthful apprenticeship to Hardy, Auden wrote:

> What I valued most in Hardy, then, as I still do, was his hawk's
> vision, his way of looking at life from a very great height, as in the
> stage directions of *The Dynasts*, or the opening chapter of *The
> Return of the Native*. To see the individual life related not only to
> the local social life of its time, but to the whole of human history,
> life on the earth, the stars, gives one both humility and self-
> confidence. For from such a perspective the difference between the
> individual and society is so slight, since both are so insignificant,
> that the latter ceases to appear as a formidable god with absolute
> rights, but rather as an equal, subject to the same laws of growth
> and decay, and therefore one with whom reconciliation is pos-
> sible.[14]

This can only mean that Auden is aware of Hardy as a presence
brooding over poems where to us he is hardly, if at all, perceptible
—for instance over the justly famous piece in *Poems, 1930:*

[13] I cannot forbear noting with a chuckle the astonishing consistency of
A. Alvarez who predictably, as it now must seem, disapproves of just those
"silted harbours" which Cleanth Brooks singles out for approval. See Alvarez,
The Shaping Spirit (London, 1958), p. 94. Alvarez's hatred for unpeopled
landscape is insatiable!
[14] W. H. Auden, "A Literary Transference," in *The Southern Review*, Vol.
VI, (1940), pp. 78-86.

> Consider this and in our time
> As the hawk sees it or the helmeted airman . . .

—in which Auden addresses the "supreme Antagonist":

> In Cornwall, Mendip, or the Pennine moor
> Your comments on the highborn mining captains,
> Found they no answer, made them wish to die
> —Lie since in barrows out of harm.
> You talk to your admirers every day
> By silted harbours, derelict works,
> In strangled orchards, and the silent combe
> Where dogs have worried or a bird was shot.

And sure enough Monroe K. Spears, examining a collection of twenty-six poems which predates even *Poems, 1930* (*Poems, 1928,* printed by Stephen Spender in Oxford), located there a Hardyesque style, laconic and in short lines, which he calls "the clipped lyric"; and he exemplifies it by some verses in which Auden already walks before us as geological topophil:

> I chose this lean country
> For seven day content,
> To satisfy the want
> Of eye and ear, to see
> The slow fastidious line
> That disciplines the fell . . .[15]

The last two lines survive into *Poems, 1930* in a poem beginning, "From scars where kestrels hover."

Spears usefully singles out two poems by Hardy written in a verse form which could have taught Auden this laconic yet lyrical style; they are "Rain on a Grave" and "In Tenebris I." Yet rather than any terseness of diction or versification, what on this showing constitutes the Hardyesque for Auden is what Auden himself points to—"his way of looking at life from a very great height."

[15] See Monroe K. Spears, *The Poetry of W. H. Auden: The Disenchanted Island* (New York, 1963), p. 23.

And in 1940 in "A Literary Transference," Auden did not shirk from pointing out the political implications of this angle of vision:

> No one who has learned to do this can ever accept either an ego-centric, overrational Humanism which fondly imagines that it is willing its own life, nor a pseudo-Marxism which rejects individual free-will but claims instead that a human society can be autonomous.

Much angry ink has been spilt on the question whether Auden in 1940 had earned the right to this lofty dismissal of alternatives by which, a few years before, he had seemed to be seduced himself. What is more to our purpose is to remark that this political statement, like others that could be read out of the early poems we have been looking at, seems much less quietistic than the logically identical statement implied by the "Bucolics."

And yet it is plain that the angle of vision of Hardy looking down from a towering height at Wessex Heights and Salisbury Plain, if it is the angle of vision from which Auden, in the "Bucolics," looks down at mountains and lakes, woods, islands and plains, is also the angle from which the young Auden had inspected the England of 1930 "as the hawk sees it or the helmeted airman." In the case of a poet so protean as Auden this constancy is remarkable. And it becomes even more striking when in his most recent collection we encounter "Amor Loci":

> I could draw its map by heart,
> showing its contours,
> strata and vegetation,
> name every height,
> small burn and lonely shieling,
> but nameless to me,
> faceless as heather or grouse,
> are those who live there,
>
> its dead too vague for judgment,
> tangible only
> what they wrought, their giant works

of delve and drainage
in days preterite: long since
their hammering stopped
as the lodes all petered out
in the Jew Limestone.

Here and there a tough chimney
still towers over
dejected masonry, moss,
decomposed machines,
with no one about, no chance
of buttering bread,
a land postured in my time
for marginal farms.

Any musical future
is most unlikely.
Industry wants Cheap Power,
romantic muscle
a perilous wilderness,
Mr. Pleasure pays
for surf-riding, claret, sex;
it offers them none.

To me, though, much: a vision,
not (as perhaps at
twelve I thought it) of Eden,
still less of a New
Jerusalem but, for one,
convinced he will die,
more comely, more credible
than either daydream.

How, but with some real focus
of desolation
could I, by analogy,
imagine a love
that, however often smeared,
shrugged at, abandoned
by a frivolous worldling,
does not abandon?[16]

---

[16] Auden, "Amor Loci," in *City Without Walls* (New York, 1969).

This poem seems to be a revision of "In Praise of Limestone,"
which, first published in 1948, was subsequently included in the
collection *Nones*. And, although that earlier poem has had many
admirers, "Amor Loci" seems to be in nearly every way an im-
provement.

Nearly every way; but not quite. For, to begin with, most readers will find "In Praise of Limestone" more entertaining. And
where Auden is concerned, this is important. For he deserves our
sympathy when he tells the poet, in a poem of 1954:

> Be subtle, various, ornamental, clever,
> And do not listen to those critics ever
> Whose crude provincial gullets crave in books
> Plain cooking made still plainer by plain cooks.[17]

Entertainment is something that we should be grateful for, from
our poets; and those critics look foolish who have refused to take
Auden seriously because he has been high-spirited, not sufficiently
glum. We may object, not to being entertained, but to being ca-
joled. And quirky cajolings have been typical of Auden's writing
from very early in his career until very recently indeed. What I
mean is something that we recognized in Betjeman—an inability
on the part of the poet to stand squarely in front of his reader, a
defensive obliquity. And there is a good deal of this in "In Praise
of Limestone," as in the slightly later "Bucolics." That said, however, it must be agreed that there is in the earlier poem a delightful
variety, a quality of invention and surprise which is present, if at
all, only in a very muted way in the fiercer and more intense
"Amor Loci."

"In Praise of Limestone" contrives, by what is really sleight of
hand, to superimpose landscapes of Ischia and even perhaps of
Greece on the limestone landscapes of Craven; in "Amor Loci"
the landscapes are those native Pennine landscapes which, as we
have seen, were the natural habitation for Auden's imagination

[17] "The Truest Poetry Is the Most Feigning," in *The Shield of Achilles* (New
York, 1955), p. 44.

from his earliest youth. With this change goes another; whereas the earlier, more expansive poem set up a "we" against a "they" (and John Fuller interestingly identifies the "we" with "intellectuals"), in "Amor Loci" there is only an "I." "We" were called "The Inconstant Ones," and it was said in the earlier poem that we responded to a limestone landscape because of the treacherous inconstancy of that kind of rock. In "Amor Loci" that treachery is registered altogether more blankly and fiercely in the astonishing phrase "the Jew Limestone." This expression must certainly give offense. For Auden to use it at a time when for instance Eliot is on every side being censured for his use of "the Jew" in "Gerontion," is an act of brutal defiance. And Auden, though in the past he has been often foolhardy and consistently impudent, has never up to this point been defiant. Auden here confronts his reader bleakly and boldly. If we compare these taut syllabics with the indulgent inclusiveness of the looping accentual lines of "In Praise of Limestone," we are compelled to realize that Auden is being graceful no longer, but intense and savage. And for this reason the modulation into the expression of Christian faith at the end of "Amor Loci" cannot help but strike us as altogether more in earnest than the corresponding modulation at the end of "In Praise of Limestone."

It is against this background of sweeping and violent change in Auden's stance and tone of voice that we must account for an unusually pointed allusion to Hardy in this poem. For such I take to be the phrase, "in days preterite." It is a phrase that I can persuade myself I have read in Hardy's *Collected Poems* (perhaps I have). At all events, it is—in its uncompromising inversion of noun and adjective and in the exact Latinate pedantry of "preterite"—unmistakably Hardyesque. In a rhetorician so adept as Auden, this does not happen by accident. And we have seen why, from Auden's point of view, a grim brief bow in Hardy's direction would seem appropriate in a poem like this which after so long reverts without equivocation to the Pennine landscape, and looks at it moreover from a height where its contours, strata, and vegetation are laid out before the poet's eye as on a map. Seen from that height, the inhabitants of the landscape are inevitably "face-less as heather or grass." And so the poem has no political implica-tions. Though it acknowledges historical perspectives (for the mining captains were gone, the Pennine slopes had reverted from heavy industry to marginal farming, already "in my time," in the bicycle age, the poet's boyhood), the poem is set outside history; because it is not concerned to make sense of historical change, it can have no political dimension—as indeed the last stanza makes clear, by insisting that the experience makes emblematic meaning only in a religious perspective.

"Amor Loci" is not of course an open-ended poem. Auden's forms—various as they are, and despite the enormous elbow room which he claims and can manage in one form after another—are always closed forms. Indeed, one may suspect that there is no call for the "open" forms, and really no possibility of using them, so long as human capacities are seen on a vertical scale from high to low. The open forms, from the time of Whitman who for our purposes invented them and first made them current, envisage man as transcending himself by moving outward and on. If he is figured as transcending himself by rising to the altitude of the hawk, or of hiding himself by delving as deep as the lowest gallery of a mine (and it is thus that Auden thinks, as does Tolkien, whom Auden is known to admire), there is every reason why poetic forms should exhibit unity, regularity, and repetition. Conversely, J. H. Prynne has earned the right to the open forms which he uses; for in Prynne's poems man saves or at least preserves himself al-ways and only by moving patiently on and over the surface of a landscape. Among the many shamanistic poems which have been such a feature of recent years in Anglo-American poetry, only Prynne's "Aristeas, in Seven Years" seems to make significant play with the profound difference in spatial relations which we encounter when we move into understanding the shamanistic reli-gions from those we are more used to, such as Christianity. For in fact it seems to be the case that the shaman's dream journey is not up or down a vertical axis as in Dante, or even in Homer, but along the level. At most, the shaman's soul, when it is conceived of as having left the body, moves up or down only in the sense of upstream or downstream—a habit of spatial perception natural enough to the hunting or pastoral nomadic cultures in which shamanism, whether in Asia or America, has been chiefly practised. (Accordingly, Prynne is right to take as his fable the epic journey of the Pontic Greek Aristeas into the Asian hinterland of Scythian and other tribes. For whereas C. M. Bowra in *Heroic Song* persuasively saw the Western epic as emerging from and superseding shamanism, the epic journey of Aristeas represents a reversal of this.)[18] If it is true that the distinction between the open-ended and the closed forms goes as deep as this, then it is doubtless true that the Hardyesque tradition in British poetry cannot after all survive a translation into the open forms; that between Hardy's precedent and Whitman's there can be no compromise. But then, of course, there can be little doubt that Thomas Hardy would have thought the Asiatic or Amerindian shaman first cousin to the witches of Endor.

[18] See E. D. Phillips, "The Legend of Aristeas: Fact and Fancy in Early Greek Notions of East Russia, Siberia, and Inner Asia," *Artibus Asiae*, XVIII, 2(1955), pp. 161-77.

～6～

A Doggy Demos:
Hardy & Lawrence

If this book had been an exercise in literary history, observing more or less choronological order, I should have had at an early stage to give attention to a number of English poets active in the 1920s who are known to have set their sights very deliberately by the model which Hardy, then still living, seemed to afford them. (Equally, I should have needed at some stage to notice how C. Day Lewis moved in the 1940s into using very explicitly Hardy-esque forms and styles.) Sydney Bolt's annotated anthology, *Poetry of the 1920s*, one of the most intelligent and valuable of recent pieces of literary criticism (though not acknowledged as such, because modestly issued as a textbook for British high schools), is the most sympathetic attempt known to me to place the poets of the 1920s in the context of their contemporaries, and to explain why the precedent of Hardy served such poets as Edmund Blunden, Siegfried Sassoon, and Robert Graves less well than the alternative models offered, though at that point hardly ever emulated, by Ezra Pound and T. S. Eliot. Bolt points out that the three poets just named, although they "all started their poetic careers under the kindly wing of Sir Edward Marsh," in the 1920s were united for a time in following, not the precepts of Edward Marsh or any other, but the precedent of Hardy. In all these poets the sensibility had been seared, and in some cases one might almost say cauterized, by their experience in the trenches of the

First World War, and they came home determined to put English poetry to the test of rendering completely and truthfully that appalling experience. Sydney Bolt's conclusion is that the precedents afforded by Hardy were inadequate to accommodate and register the horrific experiences which these poets needed to get into focus:

> The critical question was whether new tests did not demand new forms, and here the influence of Hardy was conservative. Advising the young Graves that "vers libre would come to nothing in England" he added: "all we can do is to write on the old themes in the old styles, but try to do a little better than those who went before us." The implication that the old styles were linked with old themes is clear and whether or not they recognized the fact, the themes of these poets were too new to be accommodated by minor modifications of the style they inherited. As a result, the honesty which they all had in common sometimes exposed the limitations of their verse, inviting a stylistic irony which they could not entertain. Thus, when Sassoon begins a sonnet—"When I have lost the power to feel the pang"—he invites specific comparisons with sonnets by Shakespeare, Milton and Keats which expose weakness, but which Eliot could have used as a source of sardonic strength. The only poet of the twenties who practised what he regarded as an inherited craft without exposing himself to such irony was Graves, and the reason for his immunity was, quite simply, that his version of Standard English poetry was entirely new.[1]

Sydney Bolt's contention is abundantly borne out by the poems that he prints from these authors, together with his comments upon them. (And incidentally he turns up poems by Blunden and Sassoon, both nowadays unjustly neglected writers, which are —despite the limitations which he points out—memorable and beautiful.)

When Bolt speaks of the "sardonic strength" that Eliot might have achieved out of those echoes of previous English poetry which exist in Sassoon's sonnets all too vulnerably, he is pointing to the alternative tradition, that of Pound and Eliot, which (so

[1] Sydney Bolt, *Poetry of the 1920s* (London, 1967), pp. 41-42.

he contends) would have served Sassoon and Blunden better, had they been able and ready to learn from that tradition rather than from Hardy. In Bolt's anthology Blunden, Sassoon, and Graves appear under the category "established form," while Eliot and Pound, also Yeats and (more surprisingly) William Empson, appear under the alternative rubric "dramatic form." For our purposes, and in line with terminology we have used already, for Bolt's word "dramatic" we might substitute "ironical." For in Eliot's "Prufrock" and "Gerontion," still more in Pound's *Hugh Selwyn Mauberley*, we perceive the cosmic ironies of Hardy and Housman supplanted by the strategic ironies whose later development (and decrepitude) we have seen in Betjeman and Auden. This is an important distinction to keep in mind, for cosmic irony, the ironical look on the face of the universe as it confronts man, was precisely what Sassoon and Blunden had experienced in the trenches, precisely what they wished to express in their post-war poetry. Sydney Bolt takes the point very well, speaking of Sassoon:

> Hardy's *Satires of Circumstance* was the only literary source which Siegfried Sassoon could suggest for the satirical war poems which had made him the best-known "new poet" in 1920. Indeed, his poems deserved the title more than Hardy's did. The irony of the satire does not rely upon the reader's literary tact, sense of literary tradition, or sense of values in any form: it depends upon the reader's sense of fact. Sassoon's target, in his war poetry, was cant: he exposed cant by relating it to stark reality. Reality provided the best comment. The vision of a real tank in the stalls exposes the chorus "We're sure the Kaiser loves our dear old tanks" (in "Blighters"). The spectable of "the intolerably nameless names" exposes the legend "Their name liveth for ever" on the New Menin Gate. Nothing more needs to be said.

Thus, if we describe the early poems of Eliot and Pound as "ironical," it must be clear that we mean, not the irony in a poem by Sassoon, but the strategic irony which relies upon "the reader's literary tact, sense of literary tradition, or sense of values."

In 1947, when Auden declared that "a naive rhetoric, one that is not confessedly theatrical, is now impossible in poetry," and for many years after 1947, it seemed clear that the ironical style of

Eliot and Pound had indeed conclusively superseded the relatively "naïve" rhetoric of styles derived from Hardy. But even Auden, as we have seen, was by 1970 winning through intermittently to an "honest manly style," now in the voice of Iago (see his "Song of the Devil" from *City Without Walls*), now in the voice of Thersites. And in fact time has brought in its revenges so sweepingly that the style of the early Eliot and early Pound, strategically sidestepping behind a pasteboard persona or mask, quizzing a reader always kept off balance, is nowadays heartily and intemperately disliked by readers and poets alike. This means that the issue, as between a Hardyesque style on the one hand and an Eliotic style on the other, is by no means such an open and shut case as it seemed until a few years ago. And indeed there were at least two British poets active in the 1920s whose careers as a whole would in any event have complicated the argument. One of them Sydney Bolt has acknowledged: it is Robert Graves. The other is D. H. Lawrence, who similarly emerged upon the literary scene from under the shadow of Eddy Marsh, and who similarly acknowledged Hardy as one of his masters (Whitman, however, being another).

Accordingly, since the tide changed, both these poets have been treated with a new respect—Lawrence more conspicuously than Graves. Indeed it has become possible, and not uncommon, to have Lawrence presented to us as the one honest and straightforward voice sounding to us out of the early years of this century, a voice which (so the argument goes) reveals as craven and unnecessary the "Byzantine" intricacy or "Alexandrian" evasiveness of Pound and Eliot and the poets who have followed their lead.

It is generally agreed, however, that Lawrence's verse, where it is memorable and successful, is almost all written in his own version of that *vers libre* which Hardy had declared "would come to nothing in England." In fact, it is hard to see the presence of Hardy behind any of Lawrence's worthwhile poems. And we cannot even be sure that it was Hardy who steered Lawrence, as for good or ill he steered Sassoon and Blunden, away from Eliot's and Pound's poetry of the ironical persona.

What must be our astonishment, however, to find a critic presenting Hardy as a poet who hides behind a *persona!* Yet this is just what Kenneth Rexroth maintains, urging Lawrence's superiority to Hardy on just these grounds—that whereas Hardy needed to shield himself behind an assumed mask, Lawrence didn't:

> Hardy could say to himself: "Today I am going to be a Wiltshire yeoman, sitting on a fallen rock at Stonehenge, writing a poem to my girl on a piece of wrapping paper with the gnawed stub of a pencil," and he could make it very convincing. But Lawrence really was the educated son of a coal miner, sitting under a tree that had once been part of Sherwood Forest, in a village that was rapidly becoming part of a world-wide disemboweled hell, writing hard, painful poems, to girls who carefully had been taught the art of unlove. It was all real. Love really was a mystery at the navel of the earth, like Stonehenge. The miner really was in contact with a monstrous, seething mystery, the black sun in the earth.

And again:

> Hardy was a major poet. Lawrence was a minor prophet. Like Blake and Yeats, his is the greater tradition. If Hardy ever had a girl in the hay, tipsy on cider, on the night of Boxing Day, he kept quiet about it. He may have thought that it had something to do with "the stream of his life in the darkness deathward set," but he never let on, except indirectly.[2]

This is outrageous. In part, it is meant to be. It is monstrously unfair to Hardy. But then, fairness is what we never find from any one who at any time speaks up for what Rexroth is speaking for here. Are prophets fair-minded? Can we expect Jeremiah or Amos or Isaiah to be *judicious?* Lawrence was often unfair; so were nineteenth-century prophets like Carlyle and Ruskin; so was William Blake unfair to Reynolds and to Wordsworth. And some of them, some of the time—perhaps all of them, most of the time—know that they are being unfair, as doubtless Rexroth knows it. Fair-mindedness, the prophet seems to say, is not his business; if ju-

---

[2] Introduction to *Selected Poems of D. H. Lawrence* (New York, 1959).

diciousness is necessary to society, it is the business of some one in society other than the prophet or the poet. It is Lawrence's lofty disregard for mere fair-mindedness, a loftiness readily adopted by his admirers, which makes it so difficult to be fair to him.[3]

Lawrence certainly at times assumed the mantle of a prophet, on the old-fashioned Carlylean model. But if he did, this has nothing to do with the distinction that Rexroth tries to draw between Hardy and Lawrence. The distinction as Rexroth presents it is quite simply that when "I" appears in a poem by Lawrence, the person meant is directly and immediately D. H. Lawrence, the person as historically recorded, born in such and such a place on such and such a date; whereas when "I" appears in a poem by Hardy, the person meant need not be the historically recorded Thomas Hardy, any more than when King Lear in Shakespeare's play says "I," the person meant is William Shakespeare.

When Rexroth introduces the notion of a tradition of *prophecy*, above all when he puts in that tradition the most histrionic of modern poets (W. B. Yeats), he is shifting his ground abruptly and very confusingly. What he is saying to start with is simply and bluntly that Lawrence is always sincere, whereas Hardy often isn't; and Lawrence is sincere by virtue of the fact that the "I" in his poems is always directly and immediately himself. In other words, the poetry we are asked to see as greater than Hardy's kind of poetry, though it is called "prophetic" poetry, is more accurately described as *confessional* poetry. Confessional poetry, of its nature and necessarily, is superior to dramatic or histrionic poetry; a poem in which the "I" stands immediately and unequivocally for the author is essentially and necessarily superior to a poem in which the "I" stands not for the author but for a persona of the author's—this is what Rexroth asks us to believe.

---

[3] Since I have taken issue with A. Alvarez on other topics, I ought to give credit to his temperate and persuasive and justly influential essay on Lawrence's poetry in *The Shaping Spirit* (pp. 140-61). Alvarez goes out of his way to reject Rexroth's sort of enthusiasm: "Lawrence is not a mystic; his poetry has to do with recognitions, not with revelations." It has nothing to do with "the cant of 'dark gods' " or "the stridency of *The Plumed Serpent*."

In asking us for this he is asking us, as he well knows, to fly in the face of what seemed, until a few years ago, the solidly achieved consensus about poetry and the criticism of poetry. That consensus seemed to have formed itself on the basis of insights delivered to us by the revolutionary poets of two or three generations ago. It had taken the idea of the persona from Ezra Pound, and the closely related idea of the mask from W. B. Yeats, and it had taken from T. S. Eliot the ideas that the structure of a poem was inherently a *dramatic* structure, and that the effect of poetry was an impersonal effect. It had elaborated on these hints to formulate a rule, the rule that the "I" in a poem is *never* immediately and directly the poet; that the-poet-in-his-poem is always distinct from, and must never be confounded with, the-poet-outside-his-poem, the poet as historically recorded between birthdate and date of death. To this rule there was a necessary and invaluable corollary: that the question "Is the poet sincere?"—though it would continue to be asked by naïve readers—was always an impertinent and illegitimate question. This was the view of poetry associated in America with the so-called New Criticism, and (although it has been challenged from directions other than the one we are concerned with) it is still the view of poetry taught in many classrooms.

We must now abandon it—or rather, we may and must hold by it for the sake of the poetry which it illuminates; but we can no longer hold by it as an account which does justice to *all* poetry. It illuminates nearly all the poetry that we want to remember written in English between 1550 and about 1780; but it illuminates little of the poetry in English written since. And the question has been settled already; it is only in the university classrooms that any one any longer supposes that "Is he sincere?" is a question not to be asked of poets. Confessional poetry has come back with a vengeance; for many years now, in 1972, it is the poetry that has been written by the most serious and talented poets, alike in America and Britain. Consider only the case of Robert Lowell, probably the most influential poet of his generation. It is a very telling case: trained in the very heart of New Criticism by Allen Tate,

Lowell made his reputation by poems which were characteristically dramatic monologues, in which the "I" of the poem was hardly ever to be identified with the historical Robert Lowell. Then in the mid-'50s came his collection called *Life Studies* in which the "I" of the poems nearly always asked to be taken, quite unequivocally, as Robert Lowell himself. At about the same time, from under the shadow of Rexroth himself, came Allen Ginsberg's prophetic-confessional poem, *Howl*! And ever since, confessional poems have been the order of the day, with the predictable consequences—the poem has lost all its hard-won autonomy, its independence in its own right, and has once again become the vehicle by which the writer acts out before his public the agony or the discomfort (American poets go for agony, British ones for discomfort) of being a writer, or of being alive in the twentieth century. Now we have once again poems in which the public life of the author as author, and his private life, are messily compounded, so that one needs the adventitious information of the gossip columnist to take the force or even the literal meaning of what, since it is a work of literary art, is supposedly offered as public utterance.

For these reasons, one may regret the passing of that less disheveled world in which the concept of the ironical persona was paramount. But indeed it has passed, as it had to. And yet, what has all this to do with Thomas Hardy? His reputation should have profited by this change of sentiment, as in England indeed it has. For Hardy, as we have noticed, is a thoroughly confessional poet, though his reticence about his private life concealed this to some extent until lately. What poems by Hardy could Rexroth have had in mind when he imagined the poet deciding, "I am going to be a Wiltshire yeoman. . ."? Hardy has indeed some poems which are spoken through the mouth of an imagined character, but in such cases he intimates as much very clearly, usually in his title. And much more frequently the "I" of his poems is as unequivocally the historically recorded Thomas Hardy as the "I" of Lawrence's poems is David Herbert Lawrence.

Hardy, I have contended, writes at his best when he can coerce

the painfully jangled nerves of the confessional poem into some
sort of "repose." And, little as the notion will appeal to perfervid
Lawrencians like Rexroth, the same is true of Lawrence, as he
moves from the too rawly confessional poems of his first two collections into his more mature writing of the early 1920s, in which
the repose, the saving distance, is achieved in several ways, notably
by way of emblematic fables or descriptions out of a personal
bestiary or herbal.

However, if Lawrence (and Graves also) could turn to profit
the confessional mode which Hardy bequeathed to them, only by
transcending and distancing it in ways for which Hardy provided
no precedent; if Sassoon, moreover, because he found no such way
out, thereupon ceased to be a poet of significance—it seems we
must conclude, with Sydney Bolt, that in the 1920s the models
which Hardy provided were not very useful. Eliot's ironical modes
were more fruitful. And so it looks as if the long spell of Eliot's
ascendancy as a formative influence on poets, and at the center
of an elaborately systematic criticism, was not fortuitous, nor
could it have been avoided. It was not an unnecessary aberration
from which British poetry could have escaped if it had followed a
Hardy or a Lawrence or a Graves, nor could American poetry have
been spared the expense if it had attended to William Carlos Williams.

I have spent so much time on Kenneth Rexroth because it is
worthwhile asking what animus impelled him to argue a case so
inaccurate and tendentious. And I think the answer is fairly clear:
Rexroth detects in Hardy a quality of timorousness, a sort of "cop-
out," which he dislikes and derides. Against it, what he admires
and responds to in Lawrence is a quality of risk clearly foreseen
and fearlessly taken. In Alvarez as well as in Rexroth, in all of us
to some degree, it is this in Lawrence which compels our attention,
if not always our admiration. And such a way of thinking was very
familiar to Lawrence himself throughout his career. Very early in

that career, in 1911, he reviewed an anthology of modern German poetry:

> The Germans in this book are very interesting, not so much for the intrinsic value of the pieces of poetry here given, as for showing which way the poetic spirit trends in Germany, where she finds her stuff, and how she lifts it. Synge asks for the brutalising of English poetry. Thomas Hardy and George Meredith have, to some extent, answered. But in point of brutality the Germans— and they at the heels of the French and Belgians—are miles ahead of us; or at the back of us, as the case may be.
>
> With Baudelaire, Verlaine, and Verhaeren, poetry seems to have broken out afresh, like a new crater. These men take life welling out hot and primitive, molten fire, or mud, or smoke, or strange vapour. But at any rate it comes from the central fire, which feeds all of us with life, although it is gloved, clotted over and hidden by earth and greenery and civilisation. And it is this same central well of fire which the Germans are trying to tap. It is risky, and they lose their heads when they feel the heat. But sometimes one sees the real red jet of it, pure flame and beautiful; and often, the hot mud—but that is kin. Why do we set our faces against this tapping of elemental passion? It must, in its first issuing, be awful and perhaps, ugly. But what is more essentially awful and ugly than Oedipus? And why is sex passion unsuited for handling, if hate passion, and revenge passion, and horror passion are suitable, as in Agamemnon, and Oedipus, and Medea. Hate passion, horror passion, revenge passion no longer move us so violently in life. Love passion, pitching along with it beauty and strange hate and suffering, remains the one living volcano of our souls. And we must be passionate, we are told. Why, then, not take this red fire out of the well, equally with the yellow of horror, and the dark of hate? Intrinsically, Verhaeren is surely nearer the Greek dramatists than is Swinburne.[4]

On the one hand, this reminds us that in 1911 the Hardy of the 1890s, the author of *Tess of the D'Urbervilles* and *Jude the Ob-*

[4] *The English Review*, November 1911, pp. 721-24; reprinted by Carl E. Baron, "Two Hitherto Unknown Pieces by D. H. Lawrence," in *ENCOUNTER*, August 1969, p. 4.

scure, was still to be thought of as an author who had risked a very
great deal—as he continued to do, in certain poems. On the other
hand, in 1972 can we say with any confidence that "hate passion,
horror passion, revenge passion no longer move us so violently in
life"? In any case, it gives us a valuable sense of how Lawrence at
the start of his literary career saw the challenge presented to him:
the one of his masters, Hardy, no less than the other, Whitman,
had pioneered a path of risk which it was his duty, historically, to
follow beyond the point at which they had lost heart, or had
erected a sign saying, "Thus far and no farther."

Among the risks which Lawrence saw as presented to him, as a
challenge to his poetic vocation, are certainly some which must be
called political. In view of the several sentimental and embarrassing poems which Hardy addressed to dogs or wrote about dogs, it
is appropriate to illustrate the political risks which Lawrence took,
from his poem about a bitch which he and Frieda owned in New
Mexico. The poem is called "Bibbles," and it is virulently anti-
democratic:

> And even now, Bibbles, little Ma'am, it's you who appropriated
>   me, not I you.
> As Benjamin Franklin appropriated Providence to his purposes.
>
> Oh Bibbles, black little bitch,
> I'd never have let you appropriate me, had I known.
> I never dreamed, till now, of the awful time the Lord must have,
>   "owning" humanity,
> Especially democratic live-by-love humanity.
>
> Oh Bibbles, oh Pips, oh Pipsey,
> You little black love-bird!
> *Don't* you love *everybody!*
> Just everybody.
> You love 'em all.
> Believe in the One Identity, don't you
>   You little Walt-Whitmanesque bitch?

Towards the end of the poem (so we may call it, though the
merely provisional and rhetorical disposition of line endings can

only embarrass Lawrencians who want to defend his *vers libre*),
we have:

> Me or the Mexican who comes to chop wood
> All the same,
> All humanity is jam to you.
>
> Everybody so dear, and yourself so ultra-beloved
> That you have to run out at last and eat filth,
> Gobble up filth, you horror, swallow utter abomination and
>   fresh-dropped dung.
>
> You stinker.
> You worse than a carrion-crow.
>
> Reeking dung-mouth.
> You love-bird.
> *Reject nothing*, sings Walt Whitman.
> So you, go out at last and eat the unmentionable,
> In your appetite for affection.
>
> And then you run in to vomit in my house!
> I get my love back.
> And I have to clean up after you, filth which even blind Nature
>   rejects
> From the pit of your stomach;
> But you, you snout-face, you reject nothing, you merge so much
>   in love
> You must eat even that.
>
> Then when I dust you a bit with a juniper twig
> You run straight away to live with somebody else,
> Fawn before them, and love them as if they were the ones you
>   had *really* loved all along.
> And they're taken in.
> They feel quite tender over you, till you play the same trick on
>   them, dirty bitch.
>
> Fidelity! Loyalty! Attachment!
> Oh, these are abstractions to your nasty little belly.
> You must always be a-waggle with LOVE.
> Such a waggle of love you can hardly distinguish one human
>   from another.

You love one after another, on one condition, that each one
     loves you most.
Democratic little bull-bitch, dirt-eating little swine.

And by the end of the piece the anti-democratic demand for authority becomes quite clear:

> So now, what with great Airedale dogs,
> And a kick or two,
> And a few vomiting bouts,
> And a juniper switch,
> You look at me for discrimination, don't you?
>
> Look up at me with misgiving in your bulging eyes,
> And fear in the smoky whites of your eyes, you nigger;
> And you're puzzled.
> You think you'd better mind your P's and Q's for a bit,
> Your sensitive love-pride being all hurt.
>
> All right, my little bitch.
> You learn loyalty rather than loving,
> And I'll protect you.[6]

It is intriguing to wonder how Lawrence, the author of these senti-
ments, would have responded to the loyalty of that ideal batman,
Tolkien's Sam Samwise. A related but much better poem, from
Lawrence's emblematic bestiary, is "St. Mark":

> There was a lion in Judah
> Which whelped, and was Mark.
>
> But winged.
> A lion with wings.
> At least at Venice
> Even as late as Daniele Manin.
>
> Why should he have wings?
> Is he to be a bird also?
> Or a spirit?
> Or a winged thought?
> Or a soaring consciousness?

[6] D. H. Lawrence, "Bibbles," in *The Complete Poems of D. H. Lawrence*
(New York, 1964).

Evidently he is all that,
The lion of the spirit.
Ah, Lamb of God
Would a wingless lion lie down before Thee, as this winged lion
    lies?

The lion of the spirit.

Once he lay in the mouth of a cave
And sunned his whiskers,
And lashed his tail slowly, slowly
Thinking of voluptuousness
Even of blood.

But later, in the sun of the afternoon,
Having tasted all there was to taste, and having slept his fill
He fell to frowning, as he lay with his head on his paws
And the sun coming in through the narrowest fibril of a slit in his
    eyes.

So, nine-tenths asleep, motionless, bored, and statically angry,
He saw in a shaft of light a lamb on a pinnacle, balancing a flag
    on its paw,
And he was thoroughly startled.

Going out to investigate
He found the lamb beyond him, on the inaccessible pinnacle of
    light.
So he put his paw to his nose, and pondered.

"Guard my sheep," came the silvery voice from the pinnacle,
"And I will give thee the wings of the morning."
So the lion of the senses thought it was worth it.

Hence he became a curly sheep-dog with dangerous propensities,
As Carpaccio will tell you:
Ramping round, guarding the flock of mankind,
Sharpening his teeth on the wolves,
Ramping up through the air like a kestrel
And lashing his tail above the world
And enjoying the sensation of heaven and righteousness and
    voluptuous wrath.

There is a new sweetness in his voluptuously licking his paw
Now that it is a weapon of heaven.
There is a new ecstasy in his roar of desirous love

Now that it sounds self-conscious through the unlimited sky.
He is well aware of himself
And he cherishes voluptuous delights, and thinks about them
And ceases to be a blood-thirsty king of beasts
And becomes the faithful sheep-dog of the Shepherd, thinking of
　　his voluptuous pleasure of chasing the sheep to the fold
And increasing the flock, and perhaps giving a real nip here and
　　there, a real pinch, but always well meant.

And somewhere there is a lioness.
The she-mate.
Whelps play between the paws of the lion,
The she-mate purrs.
Their castle is impregnable, their cave,
The sun comes in their lair, they are well-off,
A well-to-do family

Then the proud lion stalks abroad alone,
And roars to announce himself to the wolves
And also to encourage the red-cross Lamb
And also to ensure a goodly increase in the world.

Look at him, with his paw on the world
At Venice and elsewhere
Going blind at last.[7]

This is not exclusively nor chiefly an anti-Christian poem. It is an antiphilanthropist poem. It is directed against the do-gooder, whether he exerts himself to do good *de haut en bas* under Christian auspices or some other. In 1972 we well may think first of a militantly or complacently secular philanthropist, a Fabian expert in the behavioral sciences called in as a consultant, a social engineer, by a British or for that matter American government or municipality. What the poem is about is the devious compensation which the lion of aggressiveness can earn when he persuades himself that he is the protective sheepdog, serving the higher purpose of social cohesiveness and amelioration. The poem could be directed indeed against the Thomas Hardy who wrote poems to and for the Royal Society for the Prevention of Cruelty to Ani-

[7] From *The Complete Poems of D. H. Lawrence.*

mals. The distinctive snarling and taunting tone, here informing the disposition of free-verse lines as well as the dexterous shifts from one level of diction to another, still stings and hurts; for Lawrence's target in such a poem is just that form of government and social organization which the British have increasingly, since his death, come to accept as normal. And to set Lawrence against Hardy at this point is to raise immediately the urgent question for the modern Englishman: Do we have to accept the insistent presence of the semi-official busybody, in order to ensure what we regard as a minimal level of social and political justice? Lawrence, it is clear, wants his countrymen to answer that question with a resounding No! But of course the answer since his death has been, sometimes grudgingly and resentfully, Yes. We have given Hardy's answer, not Lawrence's.

❧

R. P. Blackmur, a critic of the Eliotic persuasion who gave a more considered account of Lawrence's poetry than any other from that inevitably hostile point of view, gives three good examples of early poems by Lawrence in which the influence of Hardy is apparent. These are "Lightning," "Turned Down," and the two quatrains called "Gypsy":

> I, the man with the red scarf,
>   Will give thee what I have, this last week's earnings.
> Take them and buy thee a silver ring
>   And wed me, to ease my yearnings.
>
> For the rest, when thou art wedded
>   I'll wet my brow for thee
> With sweat, I'll enter a house for thy sake,
>   Thou shalt shut doors on me.[8]

Blackmur remarks, "Hardy would have been ashamed of the uneven, lop-sided metrical architecture and would never have been guilty (whatever faults he had of his own) of the disturbing inner

[8] Lawrence, "Gypsy," from *The Complete Poems.*

rhyme in the second quatrain." This is true, and it is well said. It is also quite irrelevant. The whole notion of "metrical architecture," all the cluster of metaphors and analogies which lies behind such an expression, was entirely foreign to Lawrence's way of thinking about what it was he did when he wrote poems. It is not just that Lawrence rejected the architectural analogy which was so important to Hardy. He rejected also the finding of analogies for poetry in any of the other arts, including music, and insisted on the contrary, as anyone who has read even a little of him must recognize, on taking as the only reliable analogues for the act of poetic creation various biological processes of copulation, parturition, generation, metamorphosis.

This is what makes the case of Lawrence unique. It is still not pointed out sufficiently often that Lawrence's use of free verse or of "open form" is in no way a paradigm of what has been and is still normal practice in these modes. It should be plain for instance that J. H. Prynne, when he writes free verse in open form, is using a dense and elaborate rhetoric, as are those American writers such as Olson and Dorn whom Prynne is to some degree emulating. In considering these writers we can, and indeed must, talk of skill, of craftsmanship, even perhaps of "technique." Lawrence on the other hand meant just what he said in 1913 when, in a much-quoted letter, he wrote to Edward Marsh: "I have always tried to get an emotion out in its own course, without altering it. It needs the finest instinct imaginable, much finer than the skill of craftsmen"; and when a line later he exhorted Marsh to "remember skilled verse is dead in fifty years."

If we remember how necessary we found it, when speaking of Hardy's poems, to bear hard upon a distinction between "technique" and "skill," we have to say that Lawrence will tolerate poetic skill as little as poetic technique. "Technique," with its inevitably metallic and mechanical overtones in our age of technology and technocracy, is anathema to Lawrence, as it is to all free-verse poets and perhaps to all poets in our time whatever (though certainly, as I have argued, not at all so unambiguously to Hardy); but also *skill*, bringing with it a quite different range of associations (for instance with worked or incised or sculptured stone), is anathema to Lawrence no less. In Lawrence's poetry we encounter a man who is eager to junk not just industrial civilization, but also the preindustrial civilization which expressed itself in ashlar and marble, even perhaps in brick. One of the most moving of his letters, written in 1917, laments the death of the inherited English culture in images of the stonework of Garsington Manor; but Lawrence seems to have believed in all seriousness that an end had come to that culture of stonework, as it must be made to come to the culture of metal girders. To be sure, when Lawrence wrote his essay "Poetry of the Present," as his introduction to the American edition of his *New Poems,* he contrived a distinction between poetry of the past and the future, and his own poetry of the present, in such a way as to mask very engagingly the enormity of the challenge he was throwing down to his readers. But this is adroitly tactful, rather than convincing; and we have not measured up to the challenge which Lawrence throws down, we have not measured the risk which Lawrence is prepared to take with the inherited cultural goods of our civilization, if we think we can take Lawrence on Lawrence's own terms while still keeping Shakespeare or Donne unshaken in their honored niches. Lawrence would deny to such masters from the past any room at all so spacious as the generations before him had agreed to allow them. Either there are in artistic forms some kinds of fixity and finality which we are right to value as satisfying, instructive, and invigorating; or else on the contrary, as Lawrence would have us believe, there is no kind of fixity, no finality, which is other than an impediment and an obstruction to the vital apprehension which is always fluid, always in flux.

Thus Lawrence's metaphors from biology are in no way on a par with the metaphors from topography and geology which we find in Auden or in Hardy—as indeed everyone acknowledges; since no one, I think, has ever claimed Lawrence as any sort of scientific humanist. From Lawrence's extreme and exacerbated point of view, the humanistic liberal and the religious authoritarian are condemned alike and without distinction, as are all images of

strain and fixity, whether in stone or in metal. The clearest example of this is a poem called "The Revolutionary":

Look at them standing there in authority,
The pale-faces,
As if it could have any effect any more.

Pale-face authority,
Caryatids;
Pillars of white bronze standing rigid, lest the skies fall.

What a job they've got to keep it up.
Their poor, idealist foreheads naked capitals
To the entablature of clouded heaven.

When the skies are going to fall, fall they will
In a great chute and rush of débâcle downwards.
Oh and I wish the high and super-gothic heavens would come
   down now,
The heavens above, that we yearn to and aspire to.

I do not yearn, nor aspire, for I am a blind Samson
And what is daylight to me that I should look skyward?
Only I grope among you, pale-faces, caryatids, as among a forest
   of pillars that hold up the dome of high ideal heaven
Which is my prison,

And all these human pillars of loftiness, going stiff, metallic—
   stunned with the weight of their responsibility
I stumble against them.
Stumbling-blocks, painful ones.

To keep on holding up this ideal civilisation
Must be excruciating: unless you stiffen into metal, when it is
   easier to stand stock rigid than to move.

This is why I tug at them, individually, with my arm round their
   waist,
The human pillars.
They are not stronger than I am, blind Samson.
The house sways.

I shall be so glad when it comes down.
I am so tired of the limitations of their Infinite.
I am so sick of the pretensions of the Spirit.
I am so weary of pale-face importance.

Am I not blind, at the round-turning mill?
Then why should I fear their pale faces?
Or love the effulgence of their holy light,
The sun of their righteousness?

To me, all faces are dark,
All lips are dusky and valved.

Save your lips, O pale-faces,
Which are lips of metal,
Like slits in an automatic-machine, you columns of give-and-take.

To me, the earth rolls ponderously, superbly
Coming my way without forethought or afterthought.
To me, men's footfalls fall with a dull, soft rumble, ominous and
    lovely,
Coming my way.
But not your foot-falls, pale-faces,
They are a clicketing of bits of disjointed metal
Working in motion.

To me, men are palpable, invisible nearnesses in the dark
Sending out magnetic vibrations of warning, pitch-dark throbs of
    invitation.
But you, pale-faces,
You are painful, harsh-surfaced pillars that give off nothing except
    rigidity,
And I jut against you if I try to move, for you are everywhere, and
    I am blind,
Sightless among all your visuality,
You staring caryatids.

See if I don't bring you down, and all your high opinion
And all your ponderous, roofed-in erection of right and wrong,
Your particular heavens,
With a smash.

See if your skies aren't falling!
And my head, at least, is thick enough to stand it, the smash.

See if I don't move under a dark and nude, vast heaven
When your world is in ruins, under your fallen skies.
Caryatids, pale-faces.
See if I am not Lord of the dark and moving hosts
Before I die.[9]

[9] D. H. Lawrence, "The Revolutionary," from *The Complete Poems*.

It is quite beside the point that by the end Lawrence had more hopes of a revolution from the Right than from the Left; in the light of a poem such as this, his revulsion was against all forms of instituted authority whatever, and the direction from which the wind should come that would topple them from their pediments is to him almost indifferent—as indeed is acknowledged by his most enthusiastic readers today, who are most often ranged upon the political Left. Even his preference for loyalty over love—announced in "Bibbles" and developed in a poem in *Pansies* called "Fidelity" (where the rock, fidelity, is preferred to the flower, love)—is nowadays, when the revolutionary ardor of the Left is focused upon charismatic leaders like Mao and Che Guevara, as acceptable and exciting to the Left as to the Right.

But further argument is needless. If we are still a little contemptuous of Hardy's political cop-out, if we respond more vividly to Lawrence's recklessness, if we are eager to join in his condemnation of the bureaucratic philanthropist, he for his part offers us no political standing point short of wholesale and open-ended revolutionary upheaval. More even than he is a revolutionary, Lawrence is an iconoclast. *All* the graven images must be cast down and powdered—the bull of St. Luke no less than the lion of St. Mark, no less than even the biologically graven image on the horny shell of the tortoise. By the time he wrote the poem in *Pansies* called "Give us Gods," Lawrence has gone beyond all these. It is not surprising, and it is certainly not disgraceful, that English poets have refused to take that risk and pay that price.

For it needs to be asserted, now when the air is thick with voices like Rexroth's demanding that all poetry be *prophetic* (like Blake's, like Lawrence's), that prophetic poetry is necessarily an inferior poetry. The reason has emerged already. The prophet is above being fair-minded—judiciousness he leaves to some one else. But the poet will absolve himself from none of the responsibilities of being human, he will leave none of those responsibilities to "someone else." And being human involves the responsibility of being judicious and fair-minded. In this way the poet supports the intellectual venture of humankind, taking his place along with (though *above*, yet along with) the scholar and the statesman and the learned divine. His poetry supports and nourishes and helps to shape *culture*; the prophet, however, is outside culture and (really) at war with it. The prophet exists on sufferance, he is on society's expense account, part of what society can sometimes afford. Not so the poet; he is what society cannot dispense with.

Roy Fisher:
An Appreciation

Sombre mood
in the presence of things,
no matter what things;
respectful sepia.[1]

R oy Fisher's principal publications are *City* (Worcester, Migrant Press, 1961), *Ten Interiors with Various Figures* (Nottingham, Tarasque Press, 1967), *The Memorial Fountain* (New-
castle-upon-Tyne, Northern House, 1967), and *Collected Poems:
The Ghost of a Paper Bag* (London, Fulcrum Press, 1969). The
names of his publishers are significant; Fisher has published with
provincial and more or less fugitive presses, just as he has been
printed for the most part only by magazines with a limited or
specialized readership, far from the reputation-making centers of
Oxford and Cambridge and London. In the literary life of England, despite several state-instituted attempts to stimulate and
help artistic activity in the provinces, the blindness or condescension of the metropolis to writing which is provincial in its origins
or its subject matter is not much less scandalous now in the 1970s
than it was forty years ago. Fisher, like many other writers, has
suffered from this; and it is not surprising that those readers and

---

[1] Roy Fisher, "The Memorial Fountain," *Collected Poems, 1968* (Fulcrum
Press, 1969).

editors who have recognized the worth of his work should have resented how little he is known in the metropolis (and consequently outside England, for until lately the metropolitan circles had the monopoly of what English authors and reputations were promoted abroad), or that an admirable enterprise like the Fulcrum Press, when it does handsome justice to a writer like Fisher, should seem in doing so to be the organ of an underground, or a counterculture. And indeed, though "underground" and "counterculture" are both words too fashionably theatrical to be accurate, it cannot be doubted that there are in literary England two distinct circles or systems of literary activity and literary reputation, and that there is a sometimes rancorous rivalry between them. Of recent years the cause of the literary counterculture in England has been strengthened in many ways, notably by the activities of Fulcrum Press and a few similar enterprises, still more by the fact that the counterculture has established its own relations with literary activity in America, and—most momentously of all—by the fact that the most senior of England's provincial and outsider poets, Basil Bunting, has lately published what is undoubtedly his masterpiece, *Briggflatts*, by any account one of the greatest achievements of English poetry in the last forty years.

The existence of a literary culture and counterculture, of an establishment and an anti-establishment, is damaging to all English poets whatever, and obfuscating for readers of poetry. There are few enough such readers in any case; and it is gratuitously unfortunate for any poet that the small public he may hope to communicate with should be split into two halves which hardly communicate one with the other. (To give an example of the damage that is done, it is almost true to say that the full range of current American verse writing is known to no one in England, since the American writing most esteemed by the counterculture—Olson, Snyder, Levertov—is quite different from the American writing—Lowell, Berryman, Sylvia Plath—recognized and admired by the "establishment.") Moreover, as reviewers and anthologists align themselves with the one camp or the other, there is inevitably much darkening of counsel. The reader who conscientiously seeks enlightenment from these authorities will find himself being asked to take sides, and being persuaded that for instance no one can like equally Roy Fisher, who writes in free verse and in open forms, and Larkin, who characteristically uses closed forms and writes in meter. And yet this is not the case; Fisher and Larkin are very much alike, as I shall hope to show. In particular, though I think there is no evidence internal or external that Roy Fisher has ever read any of Hardy's poems with attention, his temperament is, like Larkin's, profoundly Hardyesque. If I can show this, it will support one of my principal contentions—that the Hardyesque tone in so much British writing is the result of social and political circumstances, which bear in upon and condition writers who perhaps are not directly influenced by Hardy's poems at all.

To begin with, however, what strikes the reader is the gulf between Roy Fisher's imagination and Hardy's. In an early poem, "The Intruder,"[2] Fisher, encountering suddenly the image of "a young girl. . .doing some household work, a couple of generations ago," confesses in the poem that he does not know what to do with this image, what (as it were) the image asks of him. When he says in mild bewilderment, "it's as if I had walked into somebody else's imagination," we feel that that somebody else could well have been Hardy, for whom the image of a woman thus mysteriously arising from a past scene recurred time and again to provoke some of the best poetry he ever wrote. When Roy Fisher decides, in the last line of his poem "to retire discreetly, and leave the sulky bitch to it," he is in effect refusing, with a somewhat shrill fierceness, to let his imagination walk in one of Hardy's favorite paths.

Accordingly, it comes as no surprise to find that in another early poem, "The Hospital in Winter,"[3] the attempt at rhyme and meter (those enabling constrictions so invaluable to Hardy) is quite plainly an embarrassing obstruction and impediment to Fisher, as it is in the early rhyming poems of Lawrence. And indeed, again among the early poems is one, "Why They Stopped Singing,"[4]

[2] Roy Fisher, "The Intruder." *Collected Poems.*
[3] Roy Fisher, "The Hospital in Winter." *Collected Poems.*
[4] *Collected Poems.*

which may be read as a defiant apology for abandoning such "traditional forms." The alternative open forms to which even so early Fisher vows himself are finely justified in a piece called "Linear":

> To travel and feel
> the world growing old on your body
>
> breathe and excrete
> perpetually the erosion that makes the world
>
> a caravan the little city
> that has the wit to cross a continent
>
> so patiently it cannot help but see
> how each day's dust lay and shifted and lies again
>
> no forgotten miles or kinks
> in the journey other than cunning ones
>
> to pass through many things acquisitively
> and touch against many more
>
> a long line without anything
> you could call repetition
>
> always through eroded
> country amused by others and other worlds
>
> a line like certain snail tracks
> crazily long and determined.[5]

That last image of the snail tracks might be usefully compared with the ending of "Considering the Snail," by another British poet, the scrupulous expatriate, Thom Gunn.

But the most important of Fisher's early poems is "Toyland" which, if it is worlds away from Hardy, is just as far from anything one could think of as Lawrencian:

> Today the sunlight is the paint on lead soldiers
> Only they are people scattering out of the cool church
>
> And as they go across the gravel and among the spring streets
> They spread formality: they know, we know, what they have been
> doing,

[5] *Collected Poems*. The poem is quoted in full.

The old couples, the widowed, the staunch smilers,
The deprived and the few nubile young lily-ladies,

And we know what they will do when they have opened the doors
    of their houses and walked in:
Mostly they will make water, and wash their calm hands and eat.

The organ's flourishes finish; the verger closes the doors;
The choirboys run home, and the rector goes off in his motor.

Here a policeman stalks, the sun glinting on his helmet-crest;
Then a man pushes a perambulator home; and somebody posts a
    letter.

If I sit here long enough, loving it all, I shall see the District
    Nurse pedal past,
The children going to Sunday School and the strollers strolling;

The lights darting on in different rooms as night comes in;
And I shall see washing hung out, and the postman delivering
    letters.

I might by exception see an ambulance or the fire brigade
Or even, if the chance came round, street musicians (singing and
    playing).

For the people I've seen, this seems the operation of life:
I need the paint of stillness and sunshine to see it that way.

The secret laugh of the world picks them up and shakes them like
    peas boiling;
They behave as if nothing happened; maybe they no longer
    notice.

I notice. I laugh with the laugh, cultivate it, make much of it,
But I still don't know what the joke is, to tell them.[6]

By the end of this poem, though nothing presents itself to the poet
as an alternative to what he adumbrated in "Linear," there is the
honest confession of some dissatisfaction with the inconclusive-
ness which that sort of open form brings with it.

   In his long poem, *City*, there are some sections, for instance
"The Hill Behind the Town," in which the exigencies of verse

[6] *Collected Poems*.

writing still seem to be more of a hindrance than a help to Fisher. And although this is not true of other sections in verse (for instance "The Poplars"), still the most distinguished parts of this poem— and they are very distinguished indeed—are those which are interspersed in continuous prose. For instance:

In the century that has passed since this city has become great, it has twice laid itself out in the shape of a wheel. The ghost of the older one still lies among the spokes of the new, those dozen highways that thread constricted ways through the inner suburbs, then thrust out, twice as wide, across the housing estates and into the countryside, dragging moraines of buildings with them. Sixty or seventy years ago there were other main roads, quite as important as these were then, but lying between their paths. By day they are simply alternatives, short cuts, lined solidly with parked cars and crammed with delivery vans. They look merely like side-streets, heartlessly overblown in some excess of Victorian expansion. By night, or on a Sunday, you can see them for what they are. They are still lit meagrely, and the long rows of houses, three and four storeys high, rear black above the lamps enclosing the roadways, clamping them off from whatever surrounds them. From these pavements you can sometimes see the sky at night, not obscured as it is in most parts of the city by the greenish-blue haze of light that steams out of the mercury vapour lamps. These streets are not worth lighting. The houses have not been turned into shops—they are not villas either that might have become offices, but simply tall dwellings, opening straight off the street, with cavernous entries leading into back courts.

The people who live in them are mostly very old. Some have lived through three wars, some through only one; wars of newspapers, of mysterious sciences, of coercion, of disappearance. Wars that have come down the streets from the unknown city and the unknown world, like rainwater floods in the gutters. There are small shops at street corners, with blank rows of houses between them; and taverns carved only shallowly into the massive walls. When these people go into the town, the buses they travel in stop just before they reach it, in the sombre back streets behind the Town Hall and the great insurance offices.

These lost streets are decaying only very slowly. The impacted lives of their inhabitants, the meaninglessness of news, the dead black of the chimney breasts, the conviction that the wind itself comes only from the next street, all wedge together to keep destruction out; to deflect the eye of the developer. And when destruction comes, it is total: the printed notices on the walls, block by block, a few doors left open at night, broken windows advancing down a street until fallen slates appear on the pavement and are not kicked away. Then, after a few weeks of this, the machines arrive.[7]

This is description at its most impressive, able to move with ease into analysis on the one hand and into mournful poetry on the other, and at no point subsiding into mere limp enumeration. One responds to it in the first place as one responds to Larkin's "Whitsun Weddings": this is how it is! At least, so one feels if one knows any of the industrial cities built or greatly enlarged in the nineteenth century in the English Midlands and North—cities like Leeds, Nottingham, Birmingham, Salford. The truth is, however, that not only foreign visitors to England but also many Englishmen from the Home Counties have never visited such cities; and accordingly Roy Fisher's scrupulousness is lost upon them.

It would not have been lost upon Hardy. Hardy never frequented industrial landscapes, and formally no doubt Fisher's *City* would have seemed to Hardy a very odd production indeed. Yet we can be sure that he would have responded very promptly and sympathetically to what is Fisher's central concern in this poem, the large-scale demolitions (in Fisher's Birmingham as in other industrial cities) which, gratuitously inaugurated by German bombs during the Second World War, were pursued enthusiastically through the post-war years by civic authorities. Fisher's protest against such "slum clearance," though it may owe something to what was an agitated talking-point of the 1950s, Young's and Willmott's study of the social and human implications of slum clearance in Bethnal Green[8] is thoroughly in the spirit of Hardy's address when, in 1910, he was made a freeman of the borough of Dorchester:

[7] *Collected Poems.*
[8] Michael Young and Peter Willmott, *Family and Kinship in East London* (London, 1957).

. . . An American gentleman came to me the other day in quite a bad temper, saying that he had diverged from his direct route from London to Liverpool to see ancient Dorchester, only to discover that he knew a hundred towns in the United States more ancient-looking than this (*laughter*). Well, we may be older than we look, like some ladies; but if, for instance, the original All-Saints and Trinity Churches, with their square towers, the castle, the fine mansion of the Trenchards at the corner of Shirehall Lane, the old Three Mariners Inn, the old Greyhound, the old Antelope, Lady Abingdon's house at the corner of Durngate Street, and other mediaeval buildings were still in their places, more visitors of antiquarian tastes would probably haunt the town than haunt it now. Old All-Saints was, I believe, demolished because its buttresses projected too far into the pavement. What a reason for destroying a record of 500 years in stone! I knew the architect who did it; a milder-mannered man never scuttled a sacred edifice. Milton's well-known observation in his *Areopagitica*—"Almost as well kill a man as kill a good book"—applies not a little to a good old building; which is not only a book but a unique manuscript that has no fellow.[9]

Probably none of the Birmingham buildings whose demolition is mourned by Roy Fisher reached back as far as 500 years, and (a more important point) none or few of them were in *stone*. But this does not affect the principle, which is identical in Hardy and in Fisher:

Brick-dust in sunlight. That is what I see now in the city, a dry epic flavour, whose air is human breath. A place of walls made straight with plumbline and trowel, to desiccate and crumble in the sun and smoke. Blistered paint on cisterns and girders, cracking to show the priming. Old men spit on the paving slabs, little boys urinate; and the sun dries it as it dries out patches of damp on plaster facings to leave misshapen stains. I look for things here that make old men and dead men seem young. Things which have escaped, the landscapes of many childhoods. Wharves, the oldest parts of factories, tarred gable ends rearing to take the sun over lower roofs. Soot, sunlight, brick-dust; and the breath that tastes of them.[10]

9 *The Life of Thomas Hardy, 1840-1928*, p. 352.
10 Fisher, *Collected Poems*.

It may be objected that Hardy as an architect takes it for granted, as Fisher plainly doesn't, that the buildings which are to be saved from demolition are artistically valuable, beautiful, monuments to the shaping imaginations of architects. But this is not the case, as we see quite clearly from a document of cardinal importance for understanding Hardy, his "Memories of Church Restoration," originally delivered as an address to the Society for the Protection of Ancient Buildings in 1906.[11] Here Hardy is speaking out against not literal demolition, but the more abstract and devious demolition that is called "restoration." After arguing in the first place that reproduction of an ancient feature by the restorer is an impossibility (if only because the restorer will avail himself of technical resources unknown to the original builder, since for instance "curves were often struck by hand in mediaeval work"), Hardy goes on:

> The second, or spiritual, attribute which stultifies the would-be reproducer is perhaps more important still, and is not artistic at all. It lies in human association. The influence that a building like Lincoln or Winchester exercises on a person of average impressionableness and culture is a compound influence, and though it would be a fanciful attempt to define how many fractions of that compound are aesthetic, and how many associative, there can be no doubt that the latter influence is more valuable than the former. Some may be of a different opinion, but I think the damage done to this sentiment of association by replacement, by the rupture of continuity, is mainly what makes the enormous loss this country has sustained from its seventy years of church restoration so tragic and deplorable. The protection of an ancient edifice against renewal in fresh materials is, in fact, even more of a social—I may say a humane—duty than an aesthetic one. It is the preservation of memories, history, fellowships, fraternities. Life, after all, is more than art, and that which appealed to us in the (maybe) clumsy outlines of some structure which had been looked at and entered by a dozen generations of ancestors outweighs the more subtle recognition, if any, of architectural qualities.[12]

[11] Published in *Cornhill Magazine*, July 1906. See Hardy, *Life and Art*, ed. E. Brennecke (New York, 1925).
[12] Brennecke, *Life and Art*, pp. 105-6.

It is not hard to envisage the devoted architect who might angrily denounce Hardy on this showing as, in this field as in others, a "cop-out." And in such a passage he does indeed lay himself open to the charges we have found ourselves leveling at his disciple, Larkin—of being too ready to do without distinction (artistic and other) for the sake of imaginative sympathy with the undistinguished and anonymous many. It is no more than appropriate that these sentiments should be expressed in remarkably inelegant and slipshod language. But at least the passage makes it clear that when Hardy considers the obliteration of buildings and townscapes he, no more than Roy Fisher, is concerned with the presence or absence of aesthetic quality in what is being obliterated.

On the other hand, if Hardy believes that the old is to be preserved whenever possible simply for its oldness, he is not therefore merely obstructive, sentimentally opposed to all change. In his address on receiving the freedom of Dorchester, after the tartness of "a milder-mannered man never scuttled a sacred edifice," he says surprisingly:

And when all has been said on the desirability of preserving as much as can be preserved, our power to preserve is largely an illusion. Where is the Dorchester of my early recollection—I mean the human Dorchester—the kernel—of which the houses were but the shell? Of the shops as I first recall them not a single owner remains; only in two or three instances does even the name remain. As a German author has said, "Nothing is permanent but change." Here in Dorchester, as elsewhere, I see the streets and the turnings not far different from those of my schoolboy time; but the faces that used to be seen at the doors, the inhabitants, where are they? I turn up the Weymouth Road, cross the railway-bridge, enter an iron gate to "a slope of green access," and there they are! There is the Dorchester that I knew best; there are names on white stones one after the other, names that recall the voices, cheerful and sad, anxious and indifferent, that are missing from the dwellings and pavements. Those who are old enough to have had that experience may feel that after all the permanence or otherwise of inanimate Dorchester concerns but the permanence of what is minor and accessory.

Change must come, and so must demolitions. But in every case (so Hardy seems to say) let the cost be counted—as it certainly is not counted by town-planners nor by civil engineers nor by connoisseurs of architecture and townscape, nor even by sociologists. An old church may have to be demolished; but let it be for some better reason than that "its buttresses projected too far into the pavement."

And this seems to have been what Roy Fisher meant to say in *City*. But if so, he was at that stage unable to say it clearly, because his verse writing let him down. In the midst of *City* there are for instance six lines headed, "By the Pond":

> This is bitter enough: the pallid water
> With yellow rushes crowding toward the shore,
> That fishermen's shack,
>
> The pit-mound's taut and staring wire fences,
> The ashen sky. All these can serve as conscience.
> For the rest, I'll live.[13]

And these lines (which have, incidentally, a distracting resemblance to Hardy's "Neutral Tones") cannot be understood with the help of anything elsewhere in *City*. To understand them, in particular to understand what they mean to convey by "conscience," we have to turn to a later poem called "For Realism," which evokes the scenes in the workers' streets when the local factory has discharged its shift of workers on a summer evening. On these scenes the poet comments:

> there presses in
> —and not as conscience—
> what concentrates down in the warm hollow:
>
> plenty of life there still,
> the foodshops open late, and people
> going about constantly, but not far;
>
> there's a man in a blue suit
> facing into a corner,

[13] Fisher, *Collected Poems*.

straddling to keep his shoes dry;
women step, talking, over the stream,
and when the men going by call out, he answers.

Above, dignity. A new precinct
comes over the scraped hill,
flats on the ridge get the last light.

Down Wheeler Street, the lamps
already gone, the windows have
lake stretches of silver
gashed out of tea green shadows,
the after-images of brickwork.

A conscience
builds, late, on the ridge. A realism
tries to record, before they're gone,
what silver filth these drains have run.[14]

This suggests that when, in "By the Pond," "conscience" is seen
as something apart from life, what is meant is, as in this later poem,
the social conscience of the confident demographer and humanitarian administrator who has demolished acres of the inner city
and rehoused their denizens in high-rise apartment-blocks on the
ridge above their old dwellings, at whatever cost to the human
associations that those demolished dwellings had for them. And if
this is so, other sections of *City* fall into place, as expressing, like
Lawrence's "St. Mark," distrust and dislike of the civic conscience
as embodied in the philanthropist, the officially designated do-
gooder. For instance:

At the time when the great streets were thrust out along the old
highroads and trackways, the houses shouldering towards the country and the back streets filling in the widening spaces between
them like webbed membranes, the power of will in the town was
more open, less speciously democratic, than it is now. There were,
of course, cottage railway stations, a jail that pretended to be a
castle out of Grimm, public urinals surrounded by screens of cast-
iron lacework painted green and scarlet; but there was also an arrogant ponderous architecture that dwarfed and terrified the people

14 *Collected Poems.*

by its sheer size and functional brutality: the workhouses and the older hospitals, the thick-walled abattoir, the long vaulted market-halls, the striding canal bridges and railway viaducts. Brunel was welcome here. Compared with these structures the straight white blocks and concrete roadways of today are a fair ground, a clear dream just before waking, the creation of salesmen rather than of engineers. The new city is bred out of a hard will, but as it appears, it shows itself a little ingratiating, a place of arcades, passages, easy ascents, good light. The eyes twinkle, beseech and veil themselves; the full hard mouth, the broad jaw—these are no longer made visible to all.[15]

And this is followed by a very fine evocation of a monument surviving from the city's more brutal age—a railway station; a description informed with an uneasy and unwilling nostalgia, in prose that once again is infinitely more poetic than Fisher's verse. The animus against the new breed of city fathers, who are ingratiating and paternalistic, more like salesmen than engineers, is patent. The nostalgia is for an image of naked authority, however brutal; and it is carried in images of stone.

It would be foolish to translate this into political sympathies or a political stance, arguing that Fisher wants to regain a society governed by unrestricted capitalist competitiveness. What Fisher expresses in these passages is only a mood, almost an aberration. Apart from anything else, he says, "I am not able to imagine the activity that must once have been here. I can see no ghosts of men and women, only the gigantic ghost of stone." All the same we certainly have at this point moved into the area of what we can legitimately decipher as Fisher's politics. We may deduce as much from a later poem called "Seven Attempted Moves."[16] The third of these "moves" is:

> Crisis—
>
>   a man should be able
> To hope for a well made crisis,
> Something to brace against.

[15] *Collected Poems.*
[16] *Collected Poems.*

> But see it come in rapidly and mean
> > along some corridor
> In a pauperous civic Office.

And the last of them reads:

> It is a shame. There is
> > nowhere to go.
> Doors into further in
> > lead out already
> To new gardens
> Small enough for pets' droppings
> > quickly to cover:
> Ceilings
> > too soon, steps curtailed;
> The minibed; minibath;
> > and jammed close
> > the minican.
>
> Confinement,
> > shortness of breath.
> Only a state of mind.
> > And
> Statues of it built everywhere.

The writer of these verses, in which at last the curtness of the verse-line and the choice of diction (for instance, the sardonic "It is a shame") enact the bitter distaste of the speaker, plainly is less than enthusiastic about social democracy as it has evolved in Britain since 1945. His "minibed. . .minibath. . .minican" is his way of endorsing Charles Tomlinson's angry contempt for "that suburban mental ratio which too many. . .poets attempt to impose on their experience." What is remarkable is that Fisher, unlike Tomlinson, comes by this hostile perception while restricting himself as self-denyingly as Larkin to the urbanized and industrialized landscapes of modern England.

The resemblance between Fisher and Larkin is sometimes very striking indeed. For instance, Fisher's "As He Came Near Death," one of the finest short poems to come out of England these many years, begins:

As he came near death things grew shallower for us:
We'd lost sleep and now sat muffled in the scent of tulips, the
               medical odours, and the street sounds going past,
               going away;
And he, too, slept little, the morphine and the pink light the
               curtains let through floating him with us,
So that he lay and was worked out on to the skin of his life and
               left there. . .[17]

And no one who has read Larkin with sympathy can fail to be reminded, by Fisher's fourth line, of the end of Larkin's justly admired "Afternoons," about young mothers bringing their children to play in the civic recreation ground:

> Their beauty has thickened.
> Something is pushing them
> To the side of their own lives.[18]

Behind "worked out on to the skin of his life" and "pushing them to the side of their own lives," the act of the imagination is identical. It is not, I think, anything that can be found in Hardy. And indeed Fisher at any rate seems to have had to go far afield to discover it—so far indeed that the terms "underground" and "counterculture," with their populist implications (that tedious and perennial nonsense about bringing poetry "back to the people"), are seen to be grotesquely inappropriate to his case. For he has described himself as "a 1920s Russian modernist."[19] And in fact "As He Came Near Death" ends chillingly with a fine deployment of that "making strange" which the Russian modernists found adumbrated for them already by Tolstoy:

> Then the hole: this was a slot punched in a square of plastic grass
>   rug, a slot lined with white polythene, floored with
>   dyed green gravel.

[17] *Collected Poems.*
[18] Philip Larkin, "Afternoons," in *The Whitsun Weddings.*
[19] *Contemporary Poets of the English Language,* ed. Rosalie Murphy (London and Chicago, 1970), p. 374.

> The box lay in it; we rode in the black cars round a corner, got out
>   into our coloured cars and dispersed in easy stages.
> After a time the grave got up and went away.

"Making strange," however (basically the slow-motion dismember-
ment of a ritual or routine action into its bizarre components), is
only the simplest of the devices which Fisher took over when he set
himself to school to the Russian modernists of the '20s. And when
the full battery of their resources is deployed, as in Fisher's "Three
Ceremonial Poems" or in his prose piece, *The Ship's Orchestra*
(which Edward Lucie-Smith has described—admiringly, I think—
as "perhaps the most hermetic text to have been published in England in recent years"), it seems that the game is hardly worth the
candle. Whether in English or in Russian—even in the hands of
Pasternak, who practised this mode, though infrequently—this
Russian-type modernism seems mannered and wasteful. In the
"Three Ceremonial Poems,"[20] for instance, Fisher seems to be on
the brink of making definitive judgments (about metals and stone
and urine-loosened brick as alternative media for human expression and association) which only a perverse allegiance to a non-
discursive poetics prevents him from promulgating. The "realism"
to which from time to time Fisher vows himself, seldom without
sardonic emphasis, is constantly in danger of deteriorating into the
mere enumeration of "motorbikes, dogshit, girls." And to escape
this trap (which he has always escaped in his prose, but not in his
verse), Fisher has taken this wide circuit into Mayakovsky and
Mandelstam. Yet one cannot help but remember how surely
Larkin has escaped the same pitfall, using devices no more recon-
dite than the choice epithet and the strategically reversed foot in
a metrical scheme.

Thus, although the fruits of his apprenticeship to foreign models
manifest themselves impressively in "Seven Attempted Moves" and
"As He Came Near Death," Fisher remains most challengingly the
author of *City*, imperfect as that poem is.

And, as regards the imperfections of *City*, Michael Shayer was

[20] Fisher, *Collected Poems*, pp. 76-78.

not wrong, though he was admirably bold, when he recalled in this connection the not much less manifest imperfections of *The Waste Land*, of Pound's *Cantos*, of (most pertinently) Joyce's *Ulysses*. On the one hand there is no doubt that Fisher was technically much less adroit when he embarked upon *City* than were Eliot and Pound and Joyce when severally they addressed themselves to their masterpieces. But on the other hand the terms of the problem posed were no longer the same: in the first place, the industrial metropolis could be seen by Fisher, as not by the earlier writers, as strangled by its own waste or else as built on stratum after stratum of such waste—a perception carried in *City* by Fisher's almost obsessive image of urine-loosened brick; and in the second place, the political climate had changed radically since Eliot wrote *The Waste Land* and Joyce wrote *Ulysses*:

> What follows seems to me a ruined work of art. It lies around as a series of sketches might lie around a studio waiting in vain for the total act of sculpture they were drawn to serve. Yet I am glad the writer has made no attempt to give it a bogus unity, but has preferred to leave it as it stands. What it has to say it will say to those who can see where it was aiming: if it had been tidied up the gesture it does make towards a total structure would have got obscured.
>
> Unity is hard to come by, anyway, at the depth at which this writing is operating. There are cases where love of humanity best shows itself in a desperate exposure of personal nakedness—Lear's Fool and Edgar in the storm—than in a willed uplift. The world of the last forty years is one in which whatever unity was achieved in Central Europe was at the expense of the suffering and ultimate death of six million people in concentration camps, and in which the unity of the communist world would have been impossible without the continuous presence of twenty million people in forced labour camps, and the premature death, by starvation or worse, of at least as many as were exterminated by the Germans. These things must not be forgotten in talking politics or sociology. Even in my placid area south-west of Birmingham the intake into the mental hospital is such that in a twenty-year period a fifth of the population will have had some treatment either as inpatients or outpatients. Modern industrial society seems to need its scapegoats. At their best the writers of the West have had this kind of

knowledge in their bones, and their struggles after unity can no more be written off as due to their faulty politics than can the suicides of Mayakowsky, Esenin, or Tsvetayeva.[21]

It was thus that Michael Shayer wrote about *City*, when it first appeared. It is the sort of thing that is said every day by our advertisers of apocalypse, the journalistic prophets of exciting doom who on these grounds excuse much disheveled and egotistical writing, and attack any writing which aspires to be different. If I am not disposed to put Michael Shayer in that category, it's because in the case of Fisher the struggle towards unity is so evident.

Fisher's very thorough and unsparing revision of *City* for his *Collected Poems* is further evidence of this. The two versions are very different; originally, for instance, "Toyland" was part of *City*, whereas now it is printed as an independent poem. *City* has been much improved by the revision—the prose sections, in particular, are made much tighter and cleaner. Yet some things about the poem, or behind it, emerge much more clearly when the two versions are compared. Originally, for example, the poem ended with a piece, now discarded, called "Do Not Remain Too Much Alone":

> There was a hole in the floorboards;
> I called it poetry
> Because it covered a void,
> A dusty mystery,
> And also because it had
> An orifice of form
> Whose draught about my bed
> Kept me from lying warm.

Later stanzas describe how the poet tried to fill up the hole by stuffing down it bread and sand, water and milk,

> Lead shot, nail parings, currants,
> Torn-up paper bags,
> Splinters that once were furniture
> And my clothes cut into rags;

[21] Michael Shayer, Preface to *City* (Worcester: Migrant Press, 1961), p. 3.

And so, morsel by morsel,
        Till its last trick was sprung
I poked my life away into
        The bland English tongue. . .

—whereupon, in this first version, *City* tails away in a raucous chorus:

            "O once I went a courting
                of a girl called Mary May;
            But I poked my life away boys,
                I poked my life away."

Fisher was right to eliminate this in revision (for if his poem had to remain disheveled, at least he could stop it from being egotistical); yet the image of the hole in the floor has the effect of making salient an earlier passage which in the revised version can easily be passed over inattentively, especially because in revising Fisher has pared it down and made it less explicit. I quote it in its first version:

Yet whenever I am forced to realise that some of these people around me, people I have actually seen, whose hopeful and distended surface I have at moments touched, are bodily in love and express that love bodily to dying-point, I feel that it is my own energy, my own hope, tension and sense of time in hand, that have gathered and vanished down that dark drain; that it is I who am left, shivering and exhausted, to try and kick the lid back into place so that I can go on without fear. And the terror that fills that moment or hour while I do it is a terror of anaesthesia: being able to feel only vertically, like a blind wall, or thickly, like the tyres of a bus.

Lovers turn to me faces of innocence where I would rather see faces of bright cunning. They have disappeared for entire hours into the lit holes of life, instead of lying stunned on its surface as I, and so many, do for so long, or instead of raising their heads cautiously and scenting the manifold airs that blow through the streets. Sex fuses the intersections of the web where it occurs into blobs that drag and stick; and the web is not meant to stand such weights. Often there is no web.[22]

[22] *City* (1961).

Neither here nor anywhere else in *City,* in either of its versions, is there any hint of an ironical intention, any grounds for thinking that the "I" of the poem is a persona behind which the poet conceals himself. And this makes these un-Lawrencian, indeed *anti-*Lawrencian, sentiments all the more startling. Vowed to a realism which consists of "scenting the manifold airs that blow through the streets," this is an art which sees the intensities and ecstasies of the sexual and personal life only as so many dangerous distractions. The poem is concerned with a social reality, to the exclusion of the human. And this must mean that it denies itself the possibility of tragedy, the better to render pathos. The poet is fully aware of the bargain he is striking, and he agrees to its humiliating terms. Larkin, as we have seen, lowers his sights and settles for second-best in just the same way, and just as consciously; and Hardy had sometimes done the same, though less consciously and under less provocation. Fisher's exclusion of tragedy along with ecstasy is particularly clear from a passage which in the original *City* immediately follows the passage just quoted:

> Once I wanted to prove the world was sick. Now I want to prove it healthy. The detection of sickness means that death has established itself as an element of the timetable; it has come within the range of the measurable. Where there is no time there is no sickness.

And so it comes as no surprise that the best moments in Fisher, as in Larkin, are moments of piercing pathos. Indeed "moments" gives the wrong impression; for *City* is a work of sustained pathos throughout, constructed carefully in that mode around a center—the grotesque and touching section called "Starting to Make a Tree"—in which the pathos is at its most intense.

Thus it appears that, however often Fisher may feel surges of anger at the obsequious or ingratiating meanness of the public life in his city, however he may at times hunger for more naked images of power, more monumental images of authority, more dramatic images of conflict, yet he will and does settle (with admirable consistency indeed) for Larkin's and Tolkien's hobbit-world of reduced expectations, its wistfulness regarded with an undemanding compassion. Though technically and formally Roy Fisher derives from traditions which have nothing to do with Hardy, he is a Hardyesque poet in the cast of his sensibility, or at any rate in the attitudes he takes up towards the English society that he moves in. And Michael Shayer was surely right to suggest that those attitudes, in particular Fisher's opting for pathos and compassion as his objectives, have everything to do with the history of our times, which has shown that the political alternatives to social democracy on the British model—mean-spirited as that undoubtedly is—are too costly in terms of human suffering for any man of humane feeling, least of all a poet, to find them real alternatives any longer.

~ 8 ~

A Conclusion

The flux, the endless malleability of life—have there been people in every age to whom this was the nightmare that it is for some of us today? Doubtless every age can show them, persons hungry for rigid certainties, just as every age throws up their opposites, the people for whom flux is excitement and freedom. But what is clear, surely, is that in the present century the rigidifiers are on the defensive as never before, frustrated and dissatisfied as never before; whereas the melters-down, the moulders and manipulators, the apostles of the fluid, are now in the ascendant and in the saddle. Freedom itself—not the fact of it, but the unchallengeable prestige of it as a slogan and a rallying cry that no one can afford not to rally to—is one card in the hand of the melter-down which by itself sweeps the board; once freedom is invoked, the rigidifier has to throw in his hand at once. And everything in the nature of our age conspires in the same direction; the unprecedented speed of change (technological in the first place, demanding moral and psychological change thereafter) compels anyone who has even a minimal grasp of the actual to acknowledge that the only feasible policy for him as for all others must be fluid, plastic, experimental, provisional. Yet there are people for whom this goes against the grain, who are by temperament drawn to the rigid, the hard, the resistant. For such people the present is a very hard time to live in; and the correspondence columns of any local newspaper show them protesting, crying out in pain, seeking ever more hysterical and irrational ways to break out from the impasse in which they find themselves. The more they become hysterical, as their plight forces them to envisage ever more patently foredoomed false alternatives, the more they play into their opponents' hands; and the more plausible becomes the allegation which those opponents contemptuously throw at them—that they are stupid as well as afraid, that a yearning for the rigid and the certain is to be found in any age only among the unintelligent.

Yet this is surely not the case. In another age than ours those who now seek the rigid would have settled for the stable; they would have been conservatives rather than reactionaries. For stability, in the physical and the moral universes alike, might be defined as a controllable proportion between rigid elements and fluid elements, between the persistent and the unprecedented. Nowadays what drives the naturally intelligent conservative into reactionary postures is the way in which the fluid has totally overborne the rigid, the impossibility of finding grounds for thinking that any persistent element in his life is other than an anachronistic survival, a removable impediment. Changeability seems to be total, as universal law; not only the tempo of change, but the scope of it, appears to be uncontrollable because illimitable. And in this case, the man who is stupid is not he who, however vainly, tries to resist change, but rather the many pragmatists among the apostles of change, those who think that they can ride with the wave only to that point in the future where they can stop it rolling, can alight, and can rigidify life in the momentary shape it will then have taken, a shape which conforms to their interests or their principles.

What provokes me to these reflections is thinking about sculpture. And sculpture has led others who are not sculptors into thinking along the same lines. Théophile Gautier, in "L'Art," for instance:

Tout passe.—L'art robuste
Seul a l'eternité;
     Le buste
Survit à la cité.

Et la medaille austere
Que trouve un laboureur
     Sous terre
Révèle un empereur.

Les dieux eux-mêmes meurent.
Mais les vers souverains
     Demeurent
Plus fort que les airains.

Sculpte, lime, cisèle;
Que ton rêve flottant
     Se scelle
Dans le bloc résistant![1]

For Shakespeare and many another poet before Gautier, sculptors' work in brass or bronze seemed in this way the token and the guarantee that art at any rate, the poet's no less than the sculptor's, could stem and survive the flux; that art was one element of life which persisted, changing its forms only within controllable limits, answerable to controls which were its own and embodied in its traditions. In the century since Gautier wrote, this ancient conviction has been battered and eroded; and the progressives, enamored of the flux, have been at pains to show that art forms, like all forms, are expendable, and must be thought of henceforward as provisional merely. In Michael Ayrton's novel *The Maze Maker*, the traditional assurances are given to the young sculptor Daedalus by his master:

Another time he said to me that we were the keepers of memory. "Our work will live when the warriors lie in their tombs and our work lies with them," he said. "They will be dust and what we make will lie among their bones as whole as when we made it."[2]

[1] Théophile Gautier, "L'Art."
[2] Michael Ayrton, *The Maze Maker* (London, 1967), p. 19.

But it is not clear by the end of the astonishing narrative which Michael Ayrton puts into Daedalus' mouth, whether this assurance has been vindicated. It is not what Michael Ayrton is centrally concerned with, and after all he is writing a novel, not a fable, still less a tract for the times. It is the urgency of our own concerns which makes us want to schematize it, to make an intricately rigid model out of what is tantalizingly protean.

So it is, at least if one is of those who hanker for the rigid in a world of flux. Gautier was such a one. Another was Ezra Pound, notably in a famous essay, "The Hard and the Soft in French Poetry," in which, fifty years ago, he explicitly aligned himself with Gautier. Another such was Thomas Hardy, as Edmund Blunden realized. And, if I can diagnose myself, I am another of the same kind.

In many ways Pound is the most instructive, the exemplary case, and this for all sorts of reasons. In the first place his career demonstrates all too neatly how a liking and a need for the rigid, for what he calls "the hard," may nourish at the present day extremely authoritarian politics, and of the Right, rather than the Left. Less obvious, but more intriguing, is the seeming paradox by which this poet, enamored of the hard, devotes his major poem *The Cantos* to celebrating a world of metamorphosis. Like his master Ovid, Pound, at the times when he is in control of his material in the *Cantos*, combines maximum hardness in the execution with maximum fluidity in the conception. For the world that he renders is above all things protean, malleable, in process, ceaselessly metamorphic.

And yet there is no paradox. Or if there is paradox it is one that is the very *raison d'être* of one kind of art—the art that as it happens Michael Ayrton, in his book as in his own sculptures, has chiefly been concerned with: the art of casting bronze. For those cast bronzes which Gautier and Pound respond to so eagerly, as showing how art can be durable and rigid, in fact are fashioned out of the most fluid material; the molten bronze is *poured* into the mould. The rigidity and hardness of the end product are in direct proportion to the fluid malleability in the process of production.

Most exegesis of Pound's *Cantos* is wide of the mark because by its
very nature exegesis pursues what is said, at the expense of *how* it is
said; and this means that the exegetes lead us into a world of con-
tinual flux and change which does not at all correspond to our experience as readers, of responding to the hard bright surfaces which
Pound's language, when he is in control, presents to us as a
sequence of images, each sharp-edged and distinct. The exegetes
are necessarily concerned with the process, not with the product;
with the bronze while it is still molten, not with the rigid surfaces
of the finished bust. For mythology, whether we encounter it in
the archaic records which served as source for Ovid, subsequently
for Pound, or as updated and internalized in the psychological
diagrams of Freud or Jung, is above all a fluid world, in which for
instance Hathor, Circe, and Aphrodite are only different names for
one archetypal female presence. And it is for this reason that the
man I have called the rigidifier, the devotee of the hard, the seeker
after the certain and the unchanging, is the man who will most
resist psychological explanations for art, who will most anxiously
deny that the artist is imprisoned within the maze of his own
personality, from which he can never break out to explore any
nature other than his own. For we do not need Freud or Jung to
tell us that, however the individual psyche may be in the last analysis rigidly determined by heredity or in infancy, it is, as we experience it by introspection, a realm above all protean and malleable,
a world of metamorphosis, of merging and self-transforming shapes
and fluid contours. Not in those subterranean wynds and galleries,
nor in the kneaded wax and the poured bronze which seem their
natural concomitant, shall we find what some of us will always
want more than anything else—the resistant and persisting, the
rigid and the hard, everything that poets have yearned for naïvely
in the image of the stone that resists the chisel and confronts the
sunlight.

Accordingly it is Hardy, so much the stonemason in his poetic
imagination and so resistant to the temptations of the mythological and the mythopoeic, who can seem, more than Pound, the
emblem and the exemplar in our time of what Pound meant by

"the hard" in poetry. This is not how Hardy is usually envisaged.
He is thought of as a crepuscular poet, the voice of those half-lit
hours in which phantoms and apparitions glimmer uncertainly at
the edge of vision. But this is once again to mistake the process for
the product; the poems as they lie on the page, or utter themselves
from it, speak for themselves—they are dry, angular, hard-edged.
Sometimes their angles are so sharp and so many that, as I pointed
out in Chapter 1, they make us think of industrial metalwork rather
than carved stone. And to that extent such poems are inferior to
Hardy at his best. But between stone and metal, the distinction is
not always important. Both can be images of authority, as they are,
interchangeably, in the first line of Eliot's "Coriolan":

> Stone, bronze, stone, steel, stone, oakleaves, horses' heels. . .

And the wish for the hard in art doubtless goes along with a wish
for authority in public life. Hardy satisfies both demands, the one
in fact, the other in fantasy.

Nevertheless, the prehistoric shift from the stone age to the
bronze age can still, in certain imaginative circumstances, be alive
for modern man as distinguishing at least two different kinds of
power, or even, it may be, of authority. Theorists of the Left have
pointed out for instance that once the techniques of mining and
working metals had been mastered, the way was opened towards
coinage, towards a "money economy" as opposed to a "natural
economy," and therefore to the forms of mercantile power, an
altogether more abstract sort of power since the wielder of it gives
no visible sign, for instance by any weapon that he may carry, of
possessing it. Some of the implications of this contrast have been
teased out, with a mannered terseness, by J. H. Prynne. Prynne sees
the shift from stone to metals at the start of the bronze age as a
shift from "substance" to "quality." But he hastens to qualify the
starkness of this contrast:

> That's a deliberately simplified sketch, because it may well be that
> this theorising of quality, with its control over weaponry and till-
> age and hence over life, induced a deeper cultural adherence to

substance as the zone of being in which the condition was also limit: the interior knowledge of dying. . . So that stone becomes the power substance marking the incorporated extensions of dying, and is still so as a headstone is the vulgar or common correlative of a hope for the after life.[3]

So many of Hardy's most moving poems are set in graveyards that this comment certainly seems to fit his case.

But it may well be that the modern experience can no longer define itself in the different fantasies, whether complementary or opposed, adhering to stone on the one hand, metals on the other. For it might be said that the characteristic material of modern civilization is neither stone nor metal, but composites and plastics. Certainly in both Prynne[4] and Fisher[5] we find an attempt to grapple imaginatively with the frightening perception that while the products of an industrial society may be demolished and dismembered, they cannot be destroyed. We find in them—less in what they say than in how they manipulate their medium—a recognition of what the ecology crisis has taught us to call "recycling"; that is to say, the way in which, if our civilization is not to be strangled by the detritus of its own waste products, we have to learn to live with our own waste and use that waste over and over again. Of course, to the devotee of the rigid and the hard, this vision of a world in which nothing can be destroyed though it can interminably change its shape and its function, is a new nightmare of that flux from which he continues to hope that art will save him. On the other hand, to the intelligentsia, to the moulders of opinion (that fluctuant medium which it is their interest and their nature to keep fluctuating), "ecology crisis" is a godsend; and its minatory vision of a civilization choked and poisoned by its own waste is the new stock in trade of the salesmen of apocalypse. In "The Ideal Star-Fighter," the only one of his recent poems which I think I

[3] See Prynne, "A Note on Metal," in *Aristeas* (Ferry Press, 1968), p. 14.
[4] See "L'Extase de M. Poher," in J. H. Prynne, *Brass* (Ferry Press, 1971).
[5] See Roy Fisher, *The Ship's Orchestra*, pp. 30, 36-38; and also "Three Ceremonial Songs."

understand, Prynne with just indignation rejects the moral black-
mail which the ecologist's propaganda exerts and depends upon.

Hardy's recycling poem is one that he entitles, with a typically
haughty clumsiness, "Voices from Things Growing in a Churchyard":

> These flowers are I, poor Fanny Hurd,
>   Sir or Madam,
> A little girl here sepultured.
> Once I flit-fluttered like a bird
> Above the grass, as now I wave
> In daisy shapes above my grave,
>   All day cheerily,
>   All night eerily!
>
> —I am one Bachelor Bowring, "Gent,"
>   Sir or Madam;
> In shingled oak my bones were pent;
> Hence more than a hundred years I spent
> In my feat of change from a coffin-thrall
> To a dancer of green as leaves on a wall,
>   All day cheerily,
>   All night eerily!
>
> —I, these berries of juice and gloss,
>   Sir or Madam,
> Am clear forgotten as Thomas Voss;
> Thin-urned, I have burrowed away from the moss
> That covers my sod, and have entered this yew,
> And turned to clusters ruddy of view,
>   All day cheerily,
>   All night eerily!
>
> —The Lady Gertrude, proud, high-bred,
>   Sir or Madam,
> Am I—this laurel that shades your head;
> Into its veins I have stilly sped,
> And made them of me; and my leaves now shine,
> As did my satins superfine,
>   All day cheerily,
>   All night eerily!

—I, who as innocent withwind climb,
      Sir or Madam,
Am one Eve Greensleeves, in olden time
Kissed by men from many a clime,
Beneath sun, stars, in blaze, in breeze,
As now by glowworms and by bees,
      All day cheerily,
      All night eerily!

—I'm old Squire Audeley Grey, who grew
      Sir or Madam,
Aweary of life, and in scorn withdrew
Till anon I clambered up anew
As ivy-green, when my ache was stayed,
And in that attire I have longtime gayed
      All day cheerily,
      All night eerily!

—And so these maskers breathe to each
      Sir or Madam
Who lingers here, and their lively speech
Affords an interpreter much to teach,
As their murmurous accents seem to come
Thence hitheraround in a radiant hum,
      All day cheerily,
      All night eerily!

If we think of each of these stanzas as a headstone standing in that "slope of green access" which Hardy evoked when he was given the freedom of Dorchester (though the churchyard in fact was Stinsford, not Dorchester), perhaps the symmetrical filigree of each should make us think of those eighteenth-century headstones in the old iron-mining areas of the Kentish and East Sussex Weald which are in fact not *stones* at all but iron plates. It hardly matters. The imperious energy which forced "little girl" along with "sepultured," and made that learned word cohabit through rhyme with "bird," strikes us no longer as the masterful presumption of man as technician or technologist, or else, if it does thus strike us, it is subsumed in the sense of man making what hard stay he can against the temporal flux, and (if he is technological man) using his technological symmetries and precisions to serve that perennial need.

"Cheerily". . ."eerily"—was a more eerie rhyme ever perpe-
trated? If it draws attention to itself, it draws attention only to the
yawning gulf between opposite strains of feeling, which agnostic
man must bridge, with correspondingly energetic and audacious
exertion of nervous energy, if he is to compass the fact of death.
The agnosticism, one perceives, is indeed the crux. *Ars est celare
artem*—but not when the art, and the human energy that makes
it, can rely upon nothing outside themselves to make sense of the
experience which they celebrate. By contrast, Roy Fisher's "As He
Came Near Death" relies, for its effect, upon the felt absence of a
rite which could have made death meaningful. Hardy knows on the
contrary that no rite except the one that he makes up as he goes
along will do the trick; and the solemnity of the occasion requires
that the rite thus composed be elaborate and imperiously
manipulated.

And thus it is not true that it is merely the passage of time, and
of atrocious history, which makes Roy Fisher or Philip Larkin unable to rise to Hardy's at once playful and mournful serenity. The
attainment of pathos does *not* mean the exclusion of tragedy; the
fidelity to the social need *not* mean the scanting of the human
(Fanny Hurd was a real girl called Fanny Hurden, as Hardy told
Walter de la Mare after they had walked Stinsford churchyard
together,[6] and Eve Greensleeves was Eve Trevillian or Trevelyan,
"the handsome mother of two or three illegitimate children," as
we are told in a note to the *Collected Poems*); and neither Ausch-
witz nor Katyn Forest makes the least difference to Hardy's poem.
Facing (and out-facing) death is as necessary in socialist Britain
as in capitalist America or communist Russia; and there, in the fact
of death and the term it sets to all our exertions, is the place where
we escape at last the attentions of the bureaucrats, the philanthro-
pists, and the moulders of opinion, and need the hard rigidity
which only monumental art can give us.

[6] *The Life of Thomas Hardy, 1840-1928*, pp. 413-14.

An Afterword
for the American Reader

"English poetry is presently at a very low point." Thus, in 1969, an American reviewer with respectable standards (Richard Tillinghast), writing moreover in a journal (*The Southern Review*) which has shown itself indulgent towards British writing. The English poet from whom the American reader was warned thus firmly not to expect very much was Charles Tomlinson, who has behind him twenty years of scrupulous and fiercely independent writing and verse translating on both sides of the Atlantic. Tillinghast confessed that Tomlinson "has always struck me as just another of those dull English poets." And not much in the collection he had before him (Tomlinson's *American Scenes & Other Poems*) made him want to change his mind. What *did* interest him a little was—guess what?—that Tomlinson had profited from a year in New Mexico to learn something from American poets, specifically from the late William Carlos Williams and from Robert Creeley, about how to handle free verse: "At this point Mr. Tomlinson's use of the line lacks grace and subtlety. But he has made a beginning. Perhaps Charles Tomlinson will be the one to lead his fellow countrymen out of the wilderness."

It is encouraging for the countrymen of Chaucer to realize that from the standpoint of Albuquerque they have just made a beginning, or rather have had it made for them. If I object that grace and subtlety are not necessarily the highest values in poetry, but that in any case Creeley's exquisite if pernickety melodies seem to me less graceful and subtle, as well as infinitely more restricted in range, than the tunes that Tomlinson has been playing these many years, I don't see what Tillinghast and I can do except smile and shrug and go our separate ways. And indeed we'll be lucky if we can maintain that much civility; for it looks as if, in poetry as in diplomacy, a good neighbor policy gives more offense than straightforward hostility. Anyway, it's obvious that Tillinghast is hearing what I don't hear, and vice versa.

And this is typical. One is tempted to say that for many years now British poetry and American poetry haven't been on speaking terms. But the truth is rather that they haven't been on *hearing* terms—the American reader can't hear the British poet, neither his rhythms nor his tone of voice, and the British reader only pretends to hear the rhythms and the tone of American poetry since William Carlos Williams. And so what we have had for some years now is a breakdown in communication between these two English-speaking poetries, though for civility's sake the appearance of a continuing dialogue between them is maintained.

This failure of a dialogue—the historians can explain it, as they can explain everything: which is to say, after the fact, too late to help. The American's contemptuous tolerance, the Englishman's resentful fascination—they have shown up in areas other than poetry. What is it but a reflection of the changed relationship of the English-speaking partners in other fields—in politics, in economics? And of course there is truth in this, in fact a very important and sourly paradoxical truth. For American poetry by and large has been very notably on the side of those elements in American society which most deplore American chauvinism, which reject the overweening presumption that sets out, from an unquestioned faith in American virtues, to set the world to rights; and yet American poetry is itself very chauvinistic nowadays, convinced that the rendering of American reality into poetry is a task so special that the American poet can go nowhere outside America to get assistance. This will be denied. Do not Stephen Berg and Robert Mezey, in an anthology called *Naked Poetry* (from which all British poets

are excluded), go for a title to Jimenez, and for an epigraph to
Mandelstam? Indeed they do; and doubtless it is only sour grapes
on the part of an Englishman to wonder aloud if Jimenez and
Mandelstam can be recruited so peremptorily, torn so brusquely
out of their contexts, Spanish and Russian—to wonder, in fact, if
this wholesale appropriation of foreign authorities isn't a reflection in poetry of the imperious rapacity which created just those
banana republics that American poets are ashamed of, and inveigh
against.

But there is another explanation. Culturally, the United States
remained a colony of Britain long after they had broken the
colonial ties politically and in other ways. Until well into the
present century most American writers still looked timorously to
London for appreciation and esteem. This is why, through two
generations after Whitman's death, his massive innovations were
not taken advantage of by the American poets who were his un-
grateful heirs. For the colonialist dependence of American literature upon English, already anachronistic in 1900, was artificially
protracted thereafter through the lifetime of T. S. Eliot, that
naturalized Englishman from St. Louis, Missouri, who wielded his
influence (unparalleled through the last twenty-five years of his
life) always to obscure and suppress Whitman's bequest to American writing.

And yet Eliot himself, as he acknowledged, found his feet in
poetry from study of French poets, not English ones. And this was
true, by and large, of a whole generation of American poets; as has
been noted before, American poetry came to splendid maturity in
the present century when American poets, if they needed to look
outside America for guidance, at least looked elsewhere than to
London—to Paris, to Vienna, Rapallo, even Tokyo. Vienna was
particularly fruitful. For out of Vienna came a voice which assured
the American writer that historical time could be transfigured and
displaced—and is, afresh in every generation—by Everyman (social
democracy is vindicated!) as he endures the Oedipal or some other
timeless mythical action between ego, superego, and id. Ever since,
just as diluted Marxism has been characteristic of British culture,

poetic and other, so diluted Freudianism has been characteristic of American. And at the present day this difference in allegiance, so diffused in each case that it is unconscious, accounts for one crucial difference between the English and the American poet. The Englishman supposes he is trying to operate in some highly specific historical situation, conditioned by manifold contingencies (hence his qualifications, his hesitancies, his damaging concessions), whereas the American poet, conditioned since the Pilgrim Fathers to think in utopian terms, is sure that he is enacting a drama of which the issues are basically simple and permanent, and will be seen to be so once we have penetrated through their accidental, historical overlay.

Thus what speaks in Richard Tillinghast, when he writes of Charles Tomlinson, is the voice of a post-colonialist backlash, speaking with a confidence that is all the greater for being new-found and hard-won. The Englishman, however, is not confident at all. In bad faith perhaps, spitefully and captiously, still the British poet does listen to the American voice—listens to it, listens *for* it; whereas the American poet is no longer listening to any voice but his own. And for this the British have only themselves to thank. Peter Porter, for instance, an Australian poet long resident in London, has protested that "poetry is a modest art"—a sentiment unthinkable in an American poet, or (I truly think) in any poet but a British one; and he goes on to say: "Certainly any British poet setting out to criticise American verse had better begin by acknowledging that Americans write more audaciously and commandingly than we do, even if he's sick of being told so by the Americans themselves." And British poets and critics have for years been selling the native product short in this way, freely though resentfully admitting that American poetry is more exciting and more ambitious and, well, just *better*. The most influential statement along these lines was by A. Alvarez in 1962, in an essay entitled "The New Poetry, or Beyond the Gentility Principle." This essay was Alvarez's introduction to an extraordinary anthology which he edited, called *The New Poetry*, in which eighteen British poets were mustered into line behind two Americans, John

Berryman and Robert Lowell, who were pushed to the front like drill sergeants, just to show the Britishers what they ought to have been doing and so signally weren't. Any one who reads Alvarez's essay—and it circulates widely in America, for instance in Richard Kostelanetz's symposium, *On Contemporary Literature*—can see where Berg and Mezey got the idea that "With a few exceptions (mainly Ted Hughes) nothing much new has happened in English poetry since Lawrence laid down his pen and died." And yet to a British ear, unless perhaps it is Alvarez's, the mere title of Berg's and Mezey's anthology offends against that principle which Alvarez derides as "gentility," which other Englishmen have in the past called "a sense of proportion" or even "a sense of humor." *Naked Poetry*: to many Englishmen (and I am one of them) the mere strident title is good for a giggle.

And so I come back to what is the most pervasive difference between British and American poetry nowadays, the most pervasive difference and therefore the hardest to pin down. Apparently an American reviewer of Tomlinson's *American Scenes* had complained that the poet's *persona* in the poems was that of "the considerate house guest." Richard Tillinghast, after the predictably deferential citation of Alvarez's "gentility principle," endorsed the earlier reviewer's supposedly weighty objection. And the British reader is bewildered. Would Tillinghast have preferred an *inc*onsiderate house guest? (A Dylan Thomas, perhaps?) Where does it come from, this notion that good manners in a poet are a mark against him? Is the American reader never satisfied until his poet has abused him, spat in his face, beaten him over the head? The gulf that opens here is a crucial difference of *tone*: in the poetry itself, but also in the ways of talking about it, and particularly in the poets' ways of talking about themselves as poets. The British tone is too often, too cravenly, apologetic—and the American is quite right to say that this means selling out to the philistine from the start. (In Britain the philistine is usually nowadays a humanitarian; and the British poet agrees with him in this, thus offering the extraordinary spectacle of poet and philistine combined in one person.) The American poet, when he speaks about himself and

his vocation, is too often gravely bardic and exalted—and the Englishman is quite right to say that this drives out any possibility of
self-criticism. (Or indeed of criticizing others: because all the poets
are being rapt and exalted bards together, in a sublime democracy.)

My argument has been that in surprisingly many cases in British
poetry in the last fifty years what is derided as "gentility" can be
glossed as "civic sense" or "political responsibility"; and, further,
that whether a poet should be expected to display such sense and
such responsibility is a real and open question—a question debated,
by implication, in much British verse, but hardly ever in American.
There are now on offer to the American reader anthologies of British poetry since 1945, which claim to show that British writing over
this period is as "exciting," as little "genteel," as what was being
written in America. Of the poets I have considered, it should be
plain which will be represented in such an anthology, which will
be excluded from it. Let Larkin stand as the example of those who
will be excluded. Yet, like it or not, Larkin is the centrally representative figure. And what he represents is British poetry at the
point where it has least in common with American, a poetry which
consciously repudiates the assumptions, and the liberties, which
American poets take for granted; a poetry in short which is, for the
American reader, exceptionally challenging.

Index